UNSHACKLED

HANK KIM

UNSHACKLED

A Story Unfolding Beyond the Church Walls

Copyright © 2023, 2025 by Hank Kim. All rights reserved.

No part of this book may be reproduced, stored in a retrieval system, or transmitted in any form or by any means -electronic, mechanical, photocopying, recording, or otherwise- without the express written permission of the publisher.

This is a work of non-fiction based on the author's personal experiences. In order to protect the privacy of individuals involved, certain names, characters, and locations have been changed, generalized, or omitted. The chronology and core events reflect the author's true recollections. Any resemblance to actual persons, living or deceased, is purely coincidental and unintentional.

Cover & interior design by **GW Creative LLC**
Printed in the United States of America

First edition published in **May 2023**
Revised edition published in **May 2025**

GW Creative LLC, New York

ISBN-13: 979-8-9880447-0-3

This book is dedicated to the Lord,

who has remained my faithful companion and steady light through both clarity and confusion.

To my beloved wife and daughter,

your quiet strength, patient prayers, and unwavering belief in me have carried me further than words can hold.

To my mother, whose lifelong prayers still echo in my soul,

they have been an anchor through every storm, and a quiet fire that never stopped burning.

It has been two years since this book was first released.

Much has changed. The path I thought I understood has led me deeper into questions I once avoided,

and into the humble, often hidden life of a house church,

where I've begun to reimagine what it truly means to follow Christ and be His church.

This revised edition is not a conclusion, but a continuation,

offered to those who, like me, are still searching not for a perfect faith,

but for a faithful way forward.

If you find yourself somewhere in that tension, I hope this journey meets you there.

Contents

Intro

Chapter 1: The Garden of Eden
    Note 01. Culture Shocks ──────────────── 2
    Note 02. Loyalty ──────────────── 6
    Note 03. Thirsty ──────────────── 9
    Note 04. Empathy ──────────────── 13

Chapter 2: Pandemic
    Note 05. Fear ──────────────── 20
    Note 06. Wounds ──────────────── 25
    Note 07. Scars ──────────────── 29
    Note 08. Intertwining ──────────────── 34

Chapter 3: Rituals and Practices
    Note 09. Funeral ──────────────── 40
    Note 10. Marriage ──────────────── 44
    Note 11. Appointment ──────────────── 49
    Note 12. Pastoral Visit ──────────────── 53

Chapter 4: Beyond the Church Walls
    Note 13. Forsaken ──────────────── 58
    Note 14. Revealed ──────────────── 62
    Note 15. Enlighten ──────────────── 66
    Note 16. Forsaking ──────────────── 71

Chapter 5: Unshackled
    Note 17. To the Ends of the Earth ──────────────── 76
    Note 18. Penniless ──────────────── 81
    Note 19. Consumption ──────────────── 85
    Note 20. Freedom in Truth ──────────────── 90

Introduction

In July 2020, during the height of the global pandemic, I made one of the hardest decisions of my life. For over a decade, I had devoted myself to full-time ministry, leaving behind a promising career in marketing to serve the church. I never imagined that journey would end with me walking away from the very place I had once believed I was called to build.

For a time, I served as an associate pastor at a well-known megachurch in New York City. From the outside, it looked like success. But inside, I witnessed what I can only describe as a slow unraveling both around me and within me. The deeper I stepped into the system, the more I struggled with the dissonance between the gospel we preached and the culture we practiced. Behind polished sermons and packed pews, I saw authority abused, truth diluted, and people, including myself, quietly breaking under the weight of it all.

Those final eighteen months in ministry were some of the hardest in my life. I don't use the word "failure" lightly, but that's what it felt like everything I had poured myself into had come undone. Eventually, I could no longer stay. I stepped away not because I had lost faith in God, but because I could no longer find Him in the version of church I was serving.

At first, I thought I had reached the end of my calling. But what began as an ending slowly turned into something else, a quieter, more honest search for what it means to follow Jesus. In unexpected ways, God led me toward something simpler, smaller, but more real. I found myself drawn into the life of a house church community. There, without stages or titles, I began to heal. I began to believe again.

This book is part of that journey. It is not a manifesto or a manual. It's a record of wrestling, breaking, walking away, and then being found again. I don't write to tell anyone to leave their church. I write for those who already have, or who feel they might need to. For those who love the church but can't ignore what's broken. For those who still long to be part of something sacred, even if it no longer looks like what they once knew.

If that's where you are, I hope this story meets you there.

And if you're still searching, as I am, maybe this can be a quiet companion along the way.

Chapter 1
The Garden of Eden

Unshackled: A Story Unfolding Beyond the Church Walls

Note 01
Culture Shocks

Most pastors I know begin ministry with a deep conviction and a genuine love for the church. I was no exception. Leaving behind a fifteen-year career in marketing and business wasn't something I hesitated over, not when I considered how much the Lord had already given me. To me, it felt like the least I could do: a worthy offering in response to His love.

During my decade in ministry, my family lived modestly. I served as an associate pastor at a small church in Boston, while also doing some freelance consulting on the side. My wife worked full-time to help make ends meet. It wasn't easy, not in a city like Boston, but we found our rhythm. And though our income was limited, I never complained. Every bit of support I received felt sacred, knowing it came from the honest labor and offerings of the congregation.

After ten years, I was called to serve at a large, well-known church in New York City. It felt like a major step forward something many pastors might consider a dream. I remember feeling honored and grateful, believing that my calling and efforts were being recognized. But what began as excitement would soon turn into a slow unraveling of everything I believed about the church.

On my very first Sunday as an official staff member, I was introduced at a large afternoon staff meeting following several worship services. The room was filled with dozens of pastors, team leaders, and the senior pastor himself. After brief introductions and ministry updates, the mood suddenly shifted. The senior pastor, without warning, raised his voice and began scolding the associate pastors.

The reason? No one had prayed for him during the daily morning's dawn prayer service. According to him, every public prayer, especially from the pulpit, was to include a formal petition for the senior pastor, as a sign of respect for his spiritual authority.

I remember feeling startled. Of course, I was used to praying for church leaders. It's common to intercede for pastors, staff, and the broader ministry. But this felt different. This wasn't about mutual prayer or biblical intercession. This was about formal acknowledgment, almost like an oath of allegiance. Still new to the staff and unsure of the church's internal culture, I told myself to brush it off. Maybe it was just a one-time thing. Maybe I was overreacting.

But two weeks later, that uneasy feeling came roaring back. It was my third Sunday. As usual, we gathered for the weekly staff meeting. This time, I noticed dozens of white envelopes stacked on the senior pastor's desk. One by one, he began calling out names. Each staff member stood, walked forward, bowed deeply, and received an envelope from his hand. With each handoff, the staff bowed again and thanked him repeatedly.

The envelope, I soon realized, was a paycheck. My name was called last. "This is your first paycheck," the senior pastor said with a smile, and the room responded with polite applause. I stood, bowed, accepted the envelope, and repeated "thank you" just as I had seen the others do. But inside, I was disoriented. The gesture didn't feel like appreciation, but it felt like a ritual.

At my previous church in Boston, finances were handled by the elder in charge. Staff were paid either through direct deposit or a simple check after service, no ceremony, no sense of hierarchy. But here, it was different. The senior pastor wasn't just distributing paychecks, he was positioning himself as the provider, as if the salaries flowed from his own hand. I couldn't make sense of it. Every pastoral salary, including his own, came from the tithes and offerings of the congregation, the result of their labor, sacrifice, and faith. Yet in that moment, he stood as the benefactor, receiving bows and expressions of thanks as if he were granting favor. To use the devotion of the people to elevate personal authority, and to turn what should be a humble provision into a staged display of power, was something I simply couldn't reconcile. And that subtle shift in posture, though easily overlooked, carried a symbolic weight that I couldn't ignore.

I began to notice more. Around the same time, another associate pastor was preparing to join the staff. He had been hired shortly after me but was scheduled to move from another state and begin in a few weeks. The week before his official start, he gave me a call while unpacking his things in New York. He asked if I had any insight on what ministry role he might be given. Since I had briefly heard from the senior pastor about the general direction, I offered a simple summary but advised him to confirm directly with the senior pastor for clarity.

That same afternoon, I was summoned to the senior pastor's office. He was furious. In a sharp tone, he asked, "Did you speak with the new associate pastor? What did you say?" I explained exactly what had happened, but it didn't matter. He told me I had overstepped my boundaries. According to him, the incoming pastor should not have reached out at all. His role would be assigned, not discussed. There was no room for initiative, only compliance.

A few days later, in front of the entire staff, the senior pastor announced that the associate pastor's appointment had been rescinded. No explanation. No grace. The man and his family had already moved their lives to New York. Now, just days before his official start, he was no longer welcome.

By the grace of God, that pastor later received a call from another church in the city and was able to stay. But the emotional toll of that decision, the cruelty and control embedded in it, stayed with me.

All of this happened within my first month at the church. The longer I stayed, the more I observed. Moments that felt dissonant. Practices that

stirred discomfort. Unwritten rules that reinforced loyalty, not to Christ, but to the senior pastor. I found myself returning to a question I never thought I would need to ask: "Who really leads this church?"

Scripture tells us clearly in Matthew 16:18, "I will build my church, and the gates of Hades will not prevail against it." The Church belongs to Christ. It is His body, under His lordship, guided by His Spirit. But in the environment I had entered, it seemed the true object of reverence was not Jesus, but the man in charge.

The more I reflected, the more Scripture offered contrast. 1 Peter 5:2–3 reminds us, "Shepherd the flock of God that is among you, exercising oversight, not under compulsion, but willingly… not for shameful gain, but eagerly; not domineering over those in your charge, but being examples to the flock."

But what I saw wasn't servant leadership. It was a hierarchy of fear, performance, and blind submission. Worship often felt more like a platform to promote the senior pastor's name than a space to glorify God. Authority wasn't a means to serve, it was the prize.

I wasn't angry. I was heartbroken. I had come hoping to be part of a Spirit-filled, thriving church, but instead found myself wondering if this was something that looked like a church, but had lost its heart.

In quiet moments, I thought of Jesus, not the version crafted for stage lights and slogans, but the One who knelt to wash His disciples' feet. And I saw how far we'd drifted from that vision.

These early shocks weren't just uncomfortable, they were quiet warnings. I didn't know where it would lead. But I knew I couldn't keep pretending everything was okay.

Note 02
Loyalty

Lent isn't typically emphasized in most Reformed or evangelical churches, as it's often seen as a tradition rooted in ritualistic or even pagan origins.[1] Still, some churches choose to observe it in their own way, so I wasn't particularly surprised when I heard that our church would be holding a special 40-day early morning prayer series. What did surprise me, though, was how the entire season was prepared for as if it were a major celebration.

About a week before the services began, a massive, wall-sized attendance chart listing every member of the congregation appeared in the church lobby. Pastors and staff spent hours calling church members, encouraging them to attend daily. Leading up to the start of Lent, professionally produced video promotions were shown during the worship services themselves, complete with cinematic visuals and audio, using the church's high-end broadcasting equipment. The messaging was clear: this wasn't just a spiritual discipline; it was an institutional priority.

When the first morning of Lent arrived, I stood in quiet disbelief. The parking lot was packed before sunrise, and church buses were arriving back-to-back, filled with congregants. Inside, the sanctuary was already overflowing. Those who couldn't find a seat were redirected to the basement and lobby, where the service was streamed live on large screens. The atmosphere was electric, a powerful wave of voices rising in worship and prayer. It felt less like a morning devotion and more like a

---

[1] David C. Pack, "The True Meaning of Lent," *The Restored Church of God* (https://rcg.org/articles/ttmol.html): This article explores the theory that Lent was influenced by pagan practices, and discusses how the Catholic Church adapted these traditions into the Christian observance of Lent.

revival conference.

But one moment caught my eye and refused to leave my mind. In the main lobby, before entering the sanctuary, a long table had been set up. People lined up to drop off envelopes with their names written on them into a large box. At the end of the table, a staff member entered those names into a computer. Moments later, as the worship began, the names of the donors appeared on the main sanctuary screen. Hundreds of names visible, honored, and known. Later that week, I noticed the same names printed in a special insert in the Sunday bulletin. This happened every day. And I later learned that many congregants were giving every single morning throughout the entire Lenten season.

I didn't know the amounts, and I never wanted to. But the consistency, the sheer volume of participation, stunned me. What made it even more striking was the knowledge that our church was situated in a predominantly working-class area. While not everyone was in financial need, many lived modestly. And yet, they gave daily, faithfully, often sacrificially. It reminded me of the widow Jesus spoke of in Luke 21, the one who gave two copper coins, and of whom He said, "She gave all she had."

But Jesus didn't only praise her. Just one chapter earlier, in Luke 20, He condemns the religious leaders who "devour widows' houses and for a show make lengthy prayers." Those two passages are not meant to be read in isolation. They belong together. The purity of the widow's heart and the corruption of the system that exploited her faith are part of the same painful story.[2] Jesus loved her faith. But He hated the way her devotion was used.

And that's the question that began to weigh on me, not about the people, but about the system. What does the church do with the faithful

---

[2] Richard A. Jensen, *The Widow's Offering: A Theology of Giving* (Wm. B. Eerdmans Publishing Co., 1996) 27, 33, 45, 53: Jensen's book also provides general support for the statement that Jesus rebukes the Jewish leaders who were taking advantage of the poor widow's money.

offerings of its members? During that same season, we broke ground on a second building. Massive events were being planned and held, and many of them visually stunning, packed with professional staging, sound, lighting, and video. It was not unusual for those events to be featured in local media. The church had a reputation for excellence, and we worked hard to maintain it. We were told often, "Don't worry about the budget, just make it excellent." And we did. Top-tier broadcast equipment was purchased. The sanctuary was equipped to rival a professional studio. Every Sunday felt like a televised performance, and every special occasion demanded even more.

And perhaps the congregation felt proud to see the fruit of their giving, what they had built together. It was tangible. It was impressive.

But I kept returning to a quieter question: *for whom are we building all this? Did Jesus ask for a second building? Did He require projection screens filled with donor names? Was He pleased by fame, production, and perfection?*

I couldn't say for certain. I still can't. I don't question the loyalty of the people. I saw it. I felt it. I honored it. But I struggled to discern whether all that loyalty was truly being directed to the Lord, or whether it had slowly, subtly, been redirected toward the institution that carried His name.

And that difference, between using His name and carrying His heart, became harder and harder to ignore.

Note 03
Thirsty

About a month after I officially joined the church, I noticed an announcement about a retreat being planned for a small group of young married couples. I didn't think much of it at first until I saw my name listed as the guest speaker. No one had asked me. No one had informed me. I hadn't been involved in any planning or even in conversation about the event. When I reached out to the elder overseeing the group, he explained that the church council had decided everything before I arrived. Apparently, my role was already assumed. Although I had three weeks to prepare, it was a disorienting experience like stepping into a story mid-sentence and being asked to finish the ending.

Despite the awkward start, my wife and I arrived at the retreat venue with open hearts. What we saw there surprised us. Though it was only a short, two-day gathering, the community had poured their hearts into the preparations. A generous barbecue was set up, volunteers were recruited to care for the children, and the atmosphere was full of warmth, generosity, and anticipation. It was clear that these couples were longing for something more than a break from routine. They were hungry for connection, with each other and with God.

The retreat theme was "Accompaniment," focusing on the life of Peter and his journey with Jesus. From the day he was called at the Sea of Galilee, through the intense ministry years, and his tragic denial of Christ, to the moment of restoration at the Sea of Tiberias, Peter's story became our own. We explored what it means to be followed by grace, even in failure. And what it means for Jesus to remain with us, even when we run. Each session opened space for honesty. Worship was raw and heartfelt. And by the final gathering, people were hugging, crying, and sharing words they hadn't dared to say in a long time. Many came up to me and thanked me for the message, saying they had been deeply moved. I felt proud momentarily. "Maybe I really preached well," I thought. But the more I reflected, the more I understood: it wasn't me. It wasn't the delivery, the tone, or even the content. It was the setting. The atmosphere of stillness. The absence of performance. The way God showed up when everything else fell away.

Back at the church, worship had a very different tone. Services were highly structured, carefully timed, and immaculately executed. Every transition was choreographed, and the precision left no room for interruption. 1 Corinthians 14:40, "Let all things be done decently and in order" was more than a guiding principle; it was a system. The church ran like clockwork, and every Sunday service was a production of its own. There was a kind of beauty in the seamless flow of it all, but there was also a cost.

One of the defining features of this church's worship was its use of media. Every sermon, regardless of who preached, included a video segment such as an emotional story, a visual metaphor, a professionally edited narrative that reinforced the sermon's theme. The media team operated like a studio, producing custom videos and curating content from online platforms like YouTube. These videos were powerful. They stirred emotions, drew out tears, and gave sermons a dramatic arc. In time, they became not just an enhancement but a necessity. Congregants expected it. Speakers built sermons around it. And in many ways, it worked.

But it wasn't how I preached. Over the years, I had come to embrace a different approach to preaching. Not because I was against technology or creativity, but because I was trying to protect something more essential. My sermon wasn't supposed to be a performance; it was meant to be a vessel through which God's Word could speak. In pursuit of that, I developed three simple personal rules, not as doctrine, but as discipline.

First, I aimed to keep my sermons short: never more than 20 minutes, preferably closer to 15. Second, I refused to speak beyond the scope of the text; I wouldn't inject personal arguments, speculations, or theological trends. Third, when using illustrations, I would draw from my own life whenever possible, real experiences, not borrowed examples. These weren't rules for their own sake. They were my way of keeping the message centered not on me, but on the Word. Of reducing the noise. Of clearing the stage so the spotlight could rest solely on Christ.

In a church where emotion was often orchestrated through perfectly timed transitions and cinematic media, my sermons probably felt dry or even underwhelming. I didn't include videos. I didn't follow the rhythm. I simply opened the Bible and tried to listen well, then speak carefully. And in that setting, I often felt like a foreigner.

That retreat reminded me why I preach the way I do. There were no screens. No countdowns. No video cues. Just worship and Word. Just people, stripped of pretense, meeting God together. It wasn't dramatic. It was sacred. It didn't try to impress. It invited people to breathe. And that, I realized, was what we were all thirsty for: space to be still, to be human, to be loved without distraction.

The structure of modern churches with their stages, pulpit-centered layouts, and audience-style seating, didn't originate in the early church. It came from the Roman basilica model, adopted when Christianity became the state religion. The purpose was to establish order, control, and spectacle. [3] But it replaced something far more intimate: the early church's worship around a shared table, where believers learned from one another, prayed together, and sang songs not for performance, but for presence.

---

[3] William D. Raymond, *The Basilica and the Cathedral in the Early Christian West* (Ashgate Publishing Company, 2003) 15-38: The Church adapted the basilica to meet the needs of Christian worship. It was designed to accommodate large numbers of people and featured a central aisle with a raised platform at the end.

In Colossians 3:16, Paul describes this beautifully, "Let the word of Christ dwell in you richly… teaching and admonishing one another in all wisdom, singing psalms and hymns and spiritual songs, with thankfulness in your hearts to God." There was no platform. No spotlight. Just fellowship. Just unity. Just grace moving among equals.

What we tasted at the retreat was a glimpse of that. It reminded me and everyone else of how deeply we long for worship that doesn't perform, but welcomes. That doesn't entertain, but transforms. That doesn't impress from a distance, but meets us face-to-face. The tears weren't for me. They were for the God we encountered when all the distractions were gone.

Because in the end, people aren't thirsty for better lighting or sharper videos. ***They're thirsty for God.***

And sometimes, the clearest way to meet Him is to remove everything that tries too hard to prove we already have.

Note 04
Empathy

I was given charge of a community of single young adults, most of them busy professionals trying to survive the city's relentless pace. The age range was wide, from early twenties to late thirties and even into the forties. Many didn't neatly fit the typical "young adult" mold. Some were no longer young by age, but their hearts were still searching, still asking questions that couldn't be answered by traditional church systems.

Having worked for over fifteen years in a high-pressure industry before entering ministry, I understood their burdens, not just the visible ones like long hours or tight schedules, but the inner ones: restlessness, spiritual fatigue, and the quiet fear of disconnection. These were not people who lacked faith. They simply needed a space where faith didn't feel forced, measured, or monitored. I chose to approach this ministry differently, not by telling them what to do, but by listening, praying with them, and walking beside them. And in time, a few who had once quietly drifted away came back, not because I convinced them, but because they finally felt seen.

Early on, I was warned about a particular young woman. She had once served as a leader but had developed a reputation for negativity. Other leaders said she was hard to deal with, emotionally reactive, even spiritually unstable. But when she began visiting my office regularly, I found someone completely different. Her restlessness wasn't rebellion. It was spiritual longing. She struggled with how far the church's culture had drifted from what she believed faith should be. Her honesty had made leaders uncomfortable, and because no one had listened long enough to understand her, they wrote her off.

I, too, began facing criticism for engaging with her. The senior pastor confronted me, and the former pastor and elder questioned my discernment. Eventually, the elder overseeing the ministry asked me, "Do you still want her in a leadership role? Or even in the community at all?" And then came a line I will never forget: "Pastor… why don't you just leave her behind?"

Leave her behind?

She wasn't a task to complete. She wasn't a burden to unload. She was a human being. A wounded but beautiful soul who still longed for something real. How had we come to talk about people this way as if they were objects, to be carried or discarded depending on their usefulness?

The longer I served in that church, the more I realized what it expected from its young adults. 2 Timothy 2:3–4 was often quoted: "Endure hardship with us like a good soldier of Christ Jesus… No one serving as a soldier gets involved in civilian affairs, he wants to please his commanding officer." This verse had been transformed into a framework of control. Young adults were expected to behave like soldiers: obedient, uniform, and mobilized at a moment's notice. I heard phrases like "train them," "activate them," "mobilize them," more often than I heard words like "understand them," "listen to them," or "pray with them."

Whenever a church-wide event took place, the young adult ministry was expected to show up in full force, setting up, performing, presenting, and assisting. If the numbers weren't good enough, I would get calls, pressure, and complaints. Leadership wasn't about nurturing faith. It was about visible results.

I tried to keep pace at first. I helped organize volunteers, coached team leads, even created a few structures to try and make the ministry more "efficient." But the more I tried to optimize it, the more I felt something important slipping away. These weren't resources. They weren't foot soldiers. They were sons and daughters of God carrying burdens they didn't always have the words for.

They didn't need a training program. They needed someone who could simply ask, "Are you okay?" And even if they didn't respond, they needed someone who would wait long enough for them to feel safe.

That became the heart of my ministry, not mobilizing, but listening. And in time, the ministry changed. Slowly, quietly, the community began to heal. People returned. Conversations deepened. We were no longer just managing participation, we were nurturing souls. But that wasn't the outcome the church was hoping for.

At the end of the year, I presented a report to the church council. My proposal focused not on mobilization plans or training structures, but on how the church could understand and support these young adults more deeply. I laid out ways we could build community through empathy, slow discipleship, and honest prayer. But before I could finish, the senior pastor himself stood up and threw my report to the floor.

His voice rose sharply as he said, "Are you trying to make these young people weak? Where's your system? Where's the training? Where's the mobilization plan? What exactly have you done all year?"

He wasn't simply disappointed. He was offended that I had refused to build a performance-based, militarized program that would train and deploy young adults like obedient soldiers. What he wanted was a machine. What I offered was a space for human souls.

I stood silently as he berated my lack of structure and outcomes. But inwardly, I knew what I had done.

I had stayed. I had listened.
I had refused to turn people into tools.

The following week, during the first Sunday of the new year, I was formally removed from the young adult ministry.

Some of the young people were surprised. A few texted me, quietly expressing disappointment and confusion. Others, I never heard from again. And still others perhaps the ones who had most needed gentle space fell back into silence. But I continued to pray for them. Not that they would return to a system that had wounded them, but that they would always remember: their names are known by God.

I often think of Zacchaeus. He was hated. A tax collector. His name was never spoken with kindness, only muttered with disgust in back alleys or shouted with contempt. In the eyes of the crowd, he wasn't even a person. He was a traitor. A disgrace. Just another face to avoid.

But when Jesus passed by, He didn't lecture him. He didn't tell him to repent or change or clean up his life. He simply called his name.

"Zacchaeus."

That was it.
He didn't heal him.
He didn't teach him.
He just said his name.
And for Zacchaeus, that was enough.

It had likely been years since anyone had said his name without venom. The name "Zacchaeus" had become a punchline, a curse. But when Jesus said it, something broke open. He was no longer invisible. No longer condemned. He was known."[4]

---

[4] Jacqueline Lewis, "Empathy and Zacchaeus: A Lesson from Jesus" *Journal of Religious Thought* (72(1), 2016) 69-86: Lewis argues that the story of Zacchaeus is a lesson in empathy. Jesus showed empathy for Zacchaeus by seeing him as a person, not just as a tax collector. Jesus also showed empathy by being willing to go to Zacchaeus's house, even though he knew that the people of the town would disapprove.

That's what empathy looks like. Not correcting. Not fixing. Not managing or persuading. Just saying someone's name in a way that restores their humanity. That's where ministry begins, not with strategy, but with recognition.

That final year in traditional ministry was short, but it changed everything. It was filled with pain, conflict, and disappointment. But it also held glimpses of grace, sacred silence, and quiet restoration. If I learned anything, it was this:

Empathy is not weakness.
It's what Jesus offered to Zacchaeus.
And sometimes, the holiest thing a pastor can do
is call someone by their name, not to change them,
but to remind them they've never been forgotten.

***Unshackled**: A Story Unfolding Beyond the Church Walls*

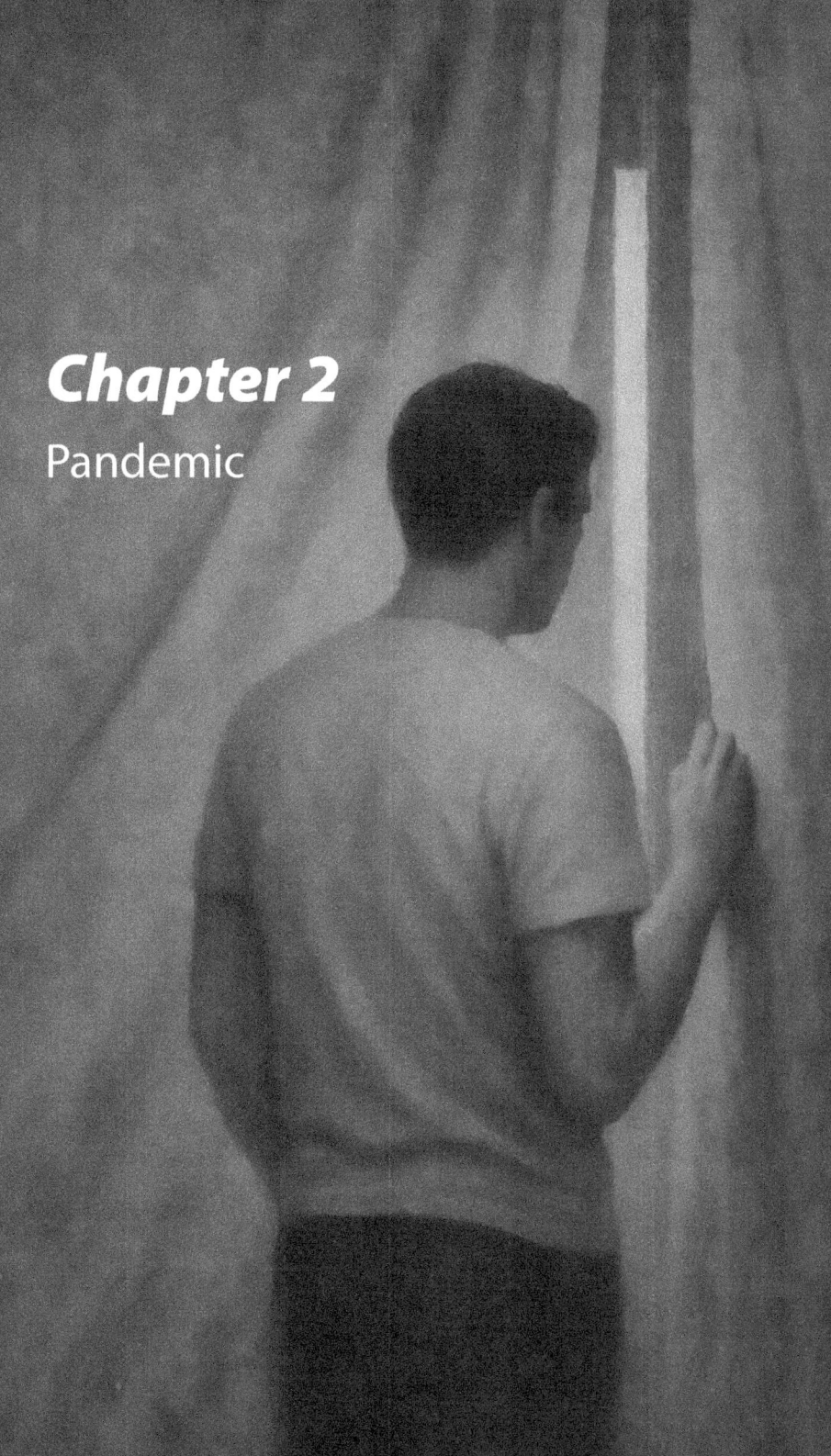

Chapter 2
Pandemic

Note 05
Fear

The fear surrounding the pandemic seemed to come out of nowhere. I received an email from my daughter's school, informing us that all students living in dormitories were required to leave and that the school would be closing. We had only three days to pack up and bring her home. With just one free day in the middle of my ministry schedule, I headed to her dormitory building, located right in front of Union Square Park in Manhattan.

The streets were packed with students and parents frantically vacating their rooms. I barely managed to load my daughter's belongings into the car as the evening sky began to dim. Then suddenly, the chaos disappeared. The streets turned eerily quiet, and we found ourselves alone in the heart of Manhattan. Not a single pedestrian or vehicle in sight. It felt like a scene straight out of a dystopian film. The view from our window was surreal, and our fear deepened in that silent drive. My wife, daughter, and I couldn't speak, and our anxiety had left us speechless.

On March 22, 2020, Governor Cuomo officially enacted a statewide executive order titled "New York State on PAUSE," marking the first full-scale lockdown in state history. But long before that date, fear had already begun spreading. Starting in late February, church staff, including myself, shifted our focus entirely to preparing for potential restrictions. As the person overseeing administration, I worked closely with our team to secure face masks, build a foundation for online worship, set up a digital giving system, and prepare the church in case a full shutdown came. Fortunately, by the time the order was issued, we had already completed much of what was needed.

Chains and padlocks were placed across the church's main entrance.

One member was seen clutching the chained doors, praying and weeping. It felt like a scene from a novel, but it was real, and it happened in New York. Our staff began contacting congregants daily to check in. Soon after, death notices began arriving one by one, mostly concerning elderly members and those in nursing homes. We were helpless. We couldn't visit. We couldn't conduct proper funerals.

One day, as I drove to the church for a quick errand, I passed by a hospital I often saw. What I witnessed was sobering. A long line of ambulances stood outside, and beside the emergency room, refrigerated trucks were lined up mobile morgues. I had seen the images on the news for days, but seeing them in person, right in my neighborhood, brought a heavy weight to my heart. The crisis was no longer a headline. It had become deeply, painfully real.

The lockdown lasted over two months. On May 15, restrictions began to ease, though only for certain industries like construction and manufacturing, and only in specific regions. In-person gatherings remained highly restricted, including church services and meetings. Despite some resistance from within the church, we complied and continued with remote worship. Services were streamed online, and clergy began meeting via Zoom and other platforms. In time, members especially older ones, adapted to the technology and began participating more easily. What started as a simple livestream gradually evolved. The media team incorporated graphics, videos, and more sophisticated production, steadily transforming our online presence.

Initially, only Sunday services were online, but soon, Bible studies, classes, and training programs also moved to video platforms. Our church had already invested heavily in media infrastructure, and now that investment paid off. Most of our regular events resumed in virtual form. Word spread quickly about our systems, and other churches in the New York area began reaching out to learn from us. The church purchased additional high-end equipment such as studio-level cameras, lighting, and audio gear. By June, we were operating like a broadcast center. Our transition had been efficient, even impressive.

But beneath the surface, other conversations were emerging.

During staff meetings and church council sessions, the most urgent discussions weren't about how people were doing emotionally or spiritually. They revolved around metrics, particularly declining video viewership and the risk of member disengagement. There was an urgency to reopen, to return to in-person worship, not only out of spiritual longing but out of fear: fear that people might leave the church for good if we waited too long.

Some leaders expressed concerns about health and safety, but they were often overshadowed by another fear, the fear of decline. In some ways, that fear seemed stronger than the fear of the virus itself.

Eventually, we overcame many challenges, and the worst of the pandemic passed. Congregants returned, and many churches resumed in-person worship. Some even experienced growth. But this wasn't the case for all. While megachurches in some regions reported larger attendance after the pandemic, countless smaller churches struggled to stay afloat, and many closed permanently. Even before the pandemic, church closures were already a serious issue with over 4,500 churches closing in 2019 in the United States alone.[5]

While the media celebrated the expansion of larger churches, national data between 2019 and 2021 showed a clear decline in church attendance and a sharp rise in the number of unchurched and unaffiliated individuals.[6] The question lingers: Were these megachurches

---

[5] Adam Gabbatt, "Losing their religion: why US churches are on the decline" *The Guardian* (January 2023, https://www.theguardian.com/us-news/2023/jan/22/us-churches-closing-religion-covid-christianity)

[6] Wendy Wang, "Here's Who Stopped Going to Church During the Pandemic" *Christianity Today* (January 2022, https://www.christianitytoday.com/ct/2022/january-web-only/attendance-decline-covid-pandemic-church.html)

truly growing by spreading the gospel, or were they merely absorbing the remaining members from smaller, failing churches?

I remembered an event our church had hosted before the pandemic: a training program called "Evangelism Explosion." It was designed to teach pastors and evangelism leaders from across the country how to share the gospel using structured methods and practical scenarios. The final service of the training featured high-resolution video projections, special effects, and even a musical performance on the main sanctuary wall. It was a massive production, and attendees were impressed by the scale and creativity.

But afterward, one pastor quietly confided in me.

"This was incredible," he said. *"But honestly, it's a bit discouraging. There's no way our small church could ever do something like this."*

That moment stuck with me. He wasn't being bitter. He was being honest. He felt that modern ministry was starting to feel inaccessible that effective evangelism now required high-end production and advanced technology. That if you couldn't stage a multimedia event, you might not be able to reach people at all.

But that's not what Scripture teaches. Romans 2:11 says, "God does not show favoritism." 1 Samuel 16:7 reminds us that "Man looks at the outward appearance, but the Lord looks at the heart." And in John 6:44, Jesus says, "No one can come to me unless the Father who sent me draws them."

Technology is helpful. Tools are valuable. But the heart of ministry has always been spiritual, not technical. When we begin to equate influence with viewership, or success with scale, we risk losing sight of what truly matters.

I still remember the thought that quietly formed in my heart as I watched all of this unfold: *"It feels like economies of scale have come to church."* Not because someone said it to me, but because it captured what I had been seeing and feeling.

It wasn't a judgment against any particular church or method. It was a moment of realization that something in our ministry culture was shifting, quietly but powerfully, and that shift had become even more visible in the wake of the pandemic.

The pandemic didn't just test our resilience. It revealed what we truly value what we fear losing, and what we're willing to compromise in order to hold onto what looks like growth.

And now I wonder, **not whether we survived as a church, but whether we truly noticed what was lost in the process.**

Note 06
Wounds

Leaving the church inflicted a deep wound on me. Practically overnight, I became someone branded, a disrupter of the church, a sinner who had brought chaos, deserving of condemnation and punishment.

This unraveling began as the government slowly lifted lockdown restrictions, and churches across New York began reopening. Within our church, two voices emerged. One called for caution, prioritizing health and safety. The other led by the senior pastor pushed for a swift and comprehensive return to normal operations. As the executive pastor under his direct supervision, I was instructed to interpret the executive orders as liberally as possible, calculating seating arrangements and space allocations in a way that would accommodate the largest number of people within legal boundaries.

But soon it became clear that the senior pastor's vision went far beyond what I had calculated, or what was permitted. He moved to reinstate activities that were still restricted by the state at the time, such as serving refreshments after service and encouraging brief indoor fellowship. While I don't fault him entirely, many churches were eager to return to in-person gatherings, and there remained a deep unease, a hesitation that lingered.

The real issue, however, wasn't about how fast we reopened or how much. It was about how these decisions were made. They were abrupt, unpredictable, sometimes decided the day before implementation, and passed directly to me as orders. There were no meetings. No dialogue. No process. In theory, as a Presbyterian church, any administrative action was to be discussed and approved by the church council. But it was clear that these were unilateral decisions. They were not being shared with the council.

One day, the clerk-elder of the council called me directly. He told me that the elders had not been consulted at all and asked if I could inform them about any new directions from the senior pastor moving forward. I agreed. To me, it seemed like a reasonable administrative request, and I didn't think twice about passing along such updates.

I didn't realize how costly that would become.

Shortly after, the senior pastor informed me that he planned to open the front yard of the church for outdoor fellowship. Following through on my word, I relayed the plan to the clerk-elder. The very next day, I was called into the senior pastor's office. He was visibly upset. He had just received a formal statement of opposition from the senior elder of the council. They considered the plan premature and unwise.

The senior pastor asked how this information had reached the council. I was stunned. I hadn't imagined that the council would push back so directly, let alone issue an official letter. In that moment of shock, I panicked and I lied. I told him I wasn't sure how they found out.

Later that day, after speaking again with the clerk-elder, I came to fully realize that it was indeed my update that had triggered the opposition. I returned to the senior pastor and explained what had happened. But it didn't matter. By then, I had already been judged as someone who had lied and disrupted church unity.

That evening, I heard that the council elders had gone to the senior pastor's home. They reportedly knelt before him, apologized, and pledged their absolute loyalty. The next day, I went to the senior pastor's office myself. I apologized, not only for the lie, but for how I had handled everything. But I couldn't apologize for the administrative process itself. I couldn't say that informing the council had been wrong. I told him I was willing to accept whatever decision the church deemed necessary.

The next day, the senior pastor asked for my resignation. I agreed. I no longer had the desire or capacity to stay. That Sunday, my resignation was announced to the congregation. The process was immediate.

It all happened so fast that I barely had time to think. It was the end of July 2020. The pandemic was still ongoing, and just like that, over a decade of ministry came to a close.

In the days that followed, I tried to make sense of everything. All I felt was shame and regret. Throughout my years in ministry, I had struggled with many aspects of the church I could not accept, and I had often gone to the Lord in prayer for discernment. But in the end, I had still chosen to act on things I did not believe in. I had prioritized the senior pastor's authority, my relationship with the elders, and the appearance of church growth over the convictions I once held.

Somewhere along the way, I had become something I never intended to be.

More than two years have passed since that day (As I work on this revised edition, five years have already passed since these events took place), but even now, recalling those events feels like reopening a raw wound. I once dreamed of becoming a pastor I could be proud of. Instead, I left in silence, humiliated, dismissed, saying goodbye to everyone I had once served.

Whenever I reflect on Jesus' abandonment, I can't help but resonate. The very people who waved palm branches crying, "Hosanna!" were the ones who shouted "Crucify Him!" And even His disciples fled.

These days, more than three years have passed since I began worshiping with a small house church community (as of April 2025). We are few in number. We have no name, no signage, no branding. For a long time, we didn't even call ourselves a church. But over time, we've come to recognize what we are. We are the church, not because of where we meet or how we're organized, but because we gather before God with sincerity and truth.

The people who gather with me each week are not strangers to wounds. Each one of them carries their own story: some of loss, some of betrayal, some of silent heartbreak at the hands of the very institution we once loved. This community began because we left the church. But slowly, it has become something more. A place not of escape, but of return. A return to what the church was meant to be.

We are still on that journey. We haven't arrived. But along the way, we've come to realize something simple and profound:

The church is not defined by its structure or its size, but by the presence of truth, grace, and the people who are willing to walk together in it.

There are no dramatic signs or wonders among us. No packed sanctuaries, no flashing lights, no programs to advertise. Only quiet worship. Shared silence. Open Bibles. And fragile hearts learning to trust again.

And in that stillness, we find life.
We are the church.
And the church is being restored in us.

Note 07
Scars

Leaving the church had happened so abruptly, it felt like the conclusion to a long and painful chapter. I thought that would be the end of the story. But it wasn't. What followed was another unraveling I hadn't anticipated.

During the early months of the pandemic, churches were scrambling to respond, not just to the virus, but to something even more destabilizing: the fear of losing members and, with them, financial support. As the executive pastor, one of my first responsibilities during lockdown was to implement systems for virtual giving. I worked quickly to set up platforms like Venmo and PayPal and explained the process to the congregation. But even with those systems in place, offerings dropped off dramatically. The news from other churches was even more disheartening, many smaller congregations couldn't pay rent, and pastors were going unpaid. In contrast, large churches with sizable reserves weathered the storm. Some even benefited from government aid. The federal Paycheck Protection Program (PPP), while intended to protect small businesses and nonprofits, disproportionately favored megachurches. I saw it firsthand. I was among those whose salaries continued without disruption.

To address the shortfall, the church created videos and announcements encouraging generosity. Parish pastors began going house to house, collecting offerings directly from members. Bit by bit, the giving returned. Alongside this, we organized relief work. We purchased and distributed essential items like masks, rice, daily side dishes, and hygiene products. We delivered lunch boxes to elderly members who lived alone and couldn't get to the market. I was tasked with publicizing these activities to local media outlets. The church frequently donated to these media channels shortly after they covered our efforts. While it was true that many people were being helped and real needs were being met, I found myself increasingly uneasy. Jesus had said, "Do not let your left hand know what your right hand is doing." Yet everything we did was being broadcast, promoted, celebrated. The charity was real, but so was the performance.

The more involved I became in the church's operations, the more I began to lose touch with my own identity as a pastor. This conflict slowly took root in my heart. When the events surrounding my resignation finally unfolded, I realized they had been long in the making.

I didn't know what I would do next. With the pandemic still raging, opportunities for new ministry were almost nonexistent. So I turned to a platform that had become central in many people's lives, YouTube. The platform wasn't unfamiliar to me. I had a degree in communications and had long been interested in media and video. It felt like a natural next step. I designed my first broadcast, chose a date for its release, and posted a short teaser video.

That teaser spread quickly. Some friends and former congregants shared it, and soon the view count began to climb. I felt a strange discomfort in response to that attention as if I had unintentionally crossed a line I hadn't yet understood.

A few days before the premiere, I got a call from the clerk of our local presbytery. He informed me that the presbytery had convened and voted to discipline me for launching the YouTube channel even though I had already officially resigned from my church post. I was no longer a pastor of the church, no longer on staff, yet I was being summoned to account for my personal decision to share the gospel online.

What made it worse was the political structure behind the scenes. At the time, my former senior pastor was also serving as moderator of the presbytery. He held the highest office both inside our church and within the governing body that oversaw me even after I had left. That dual role gave him enormous influence, and I had no institutional support, no community, and no voice to push back.

I was just one person.

And now I was being summoned before a group of pastors who were still under his leadership.

When I arrived at the church for the meeting, the atmosphere was cold and clinical. The ministers of the presbytery sat lined up in a row. I was placed at the opposite end of the table alone. It felt less like a meeting and more like a trial. And I was not there to speak. I was there to listen. To be rebuked. To be silenced.

At one point, one of the pastors asked me, "Whose word will you obey, your senior pastor's or Jesus'?"

I blinked in disbelief. Before I could respond, he continued, "When the founding pastor of this church hired new associate pastors, he would ask that same question. And only those who said they would obey the senior pastor were hired. That's still our standard."

The others nodded in agreement. In that moment, something clicked. All the strange events I had experienced during my time at the church such as sudden decisions, controlling leadership, unquestioned authority, they all made sense now.

They handed me a printed confession statement. I hadn't written it. I didn't agree with it. But they told me to sign. And I did. Not because I agreed, but because I felt cornered.

I was no longer a pastor. No longer part of the system.

But I was still being treated like its property, like I was being held as collateral by an institution I had already left.

I walked out of the building with a lump in my throat.
That evening, I shut down my YouTube channel.
And that day left one of the deepest scars I carry to this day.

The very next morning, at the church's dawn prayer service, the senior pastor reportedly gave a sermon filled with public condemnation directed at me. Though I didn't attend and didn't hear the message myself, the phone calls began pouring in. Friends and acquaintances called to comfort me. Most of those calls were answered by my wife. I sat in silence, unable to process what I hadn't even heard firsthand. But the echo of those words, carried to me through others, hurt just the same. Another scar. Another wound, inflicted not in a quiet office, but from the pulpit before an entire congregation.

But not all my memories are wounds.
Some are painful and beautiful at the same time.

In 2019, before the pandemic, a tragedy struck a family in our congregation. Their young daughter had drowned in a backyard pool. The loss devastated us all. That Sunday, in the absence of the senior pastor, I was asked to preach. I didn't know what to say. How could I explain such grief?

After much prayer, I was led to John 4, the story of the Samaritan woman. She is often misunderstood. Many label her as sinful, but I saw her as wounded. In that time, a woman couldn't file for divorce. Which meant that she had likely been discarded again and again. Her life was one long series of rejections. Until she met Jesus.[7] What struck me most

---

[7] Catherine Kroeger, *The Woman at the Well: A Different Look* (Augsburg Fortress. 1992) Chapter 5: Kroeger argues that the woman's multiple marriages and current living arrangement with a man who was not her husband were not necessarily indicative of her own immorality, but rather the result of a patriarchal society in which women had little agency and could easily be abandoned by their husbands. Kroeger draws on historical and cultural context to paint a more sympathetic picture of the woman, and to suggest that her encounter with Jesus was a transformative moment that allowed her to move beyond the shame and marginalization she had experienced.

was that Jesus didn't heal her wounds. He didn't promise her a solution. He didn't offer comfort in the traditional sense. He simply said, "I am He." That one line was enough. It restored her identity. It revived her hope. And she stood up.

I have often found myself like that woman, asking, "Why, Lord? Why did this happen? Why me?" But sometimes, the answer doesn't come in the form of an explanation. Sometimes it's just presence. Just the quiet voice that says, "I am He."

> *Some wounds become scars, permanent reminders of pain.*
> *Others heal and fade.*
> *Mine are still visible.*
> *But like the woman at Sychar, I am learning to live with them.*
> *And even in the broken places, faith can grow.*

Unshackled: A Story Unfolding Beyond the Church Walls

Note 08
Intertwining

One of the starkest contrasts I noticed upon entering a megachurch was the sheer number of employees. In most small and medium-sized churches, the only staff typically includes a senior pastor, a few associate pastors, and perhaps one administrative assistant. But in this church, I had to adjust to an entirely different reality. There were dozens of full-time employees: receptionists, secretaries, conductors, soloists, musicians, media technicians, janitors, cleaners, chefs, and more. There were departments handling publishing, event operations, online retail, and internal communication. The church also maintained direct relationships with contractors managing its utilities: heating, cooling, plumbing, electric work. It even had internal food supply lines and equipment vendors, many of which were managed by or tied to church members and their families.

At first, it all seemed like the natural result of ministry expansion. I assumed such organizational complexity was necessary for the scale of ministry they handled. And from the outside, it seemed impressive, efficient, organized, and visionary. But slowly, I began to realize something deeper was at play.

As I got to know the congregation, I discovered that many members were directly or indirectly financially tied to the church. Some ran businesses that served the church as vendors. Some received referrals. Others were employed by various affiliated entities or volunteered in ways that mimicked employment. The boundaries between spiritual community and economic ecosystem were blurry. On the surface, it resembled the "all things in common" spirit from

Acts 2:44–45, where early believers shared possessions and supported each other's needs.[8] But this was different. This wasn't self-sacrificial generosity. It was a web of mutual dependencies, where spiritual loyalty and economic benefit often overlapped.

In this tightly woven system, dissent felt dangerous.

The deeper I got involved in leadership, the more I understood how this intertwining created a strong internal cohesion. People weren't just bound by faith or shared mission. They were bound by contracts, expectations, and reputational currency. Loyalty wasn't only spiritual; it was structural. And structure, once built, becomes very difficult to challenge.

One day, the church launched a new initiative, an online shopping mall that sold Christian-themed merchandise, including apparel with Bible verses. The platform was quickly built using internal teams, and the children of members were even used as clothing models. Church members with connections in fashion and design helped with product development and branding. On the surface, it looked like a wonderful, creative way to express faith and support the church.

But not everyone felt that way. A few elders quietly opposed the project, questioning the ethical implications of mixing ministry with business. They feared this was a step too far, a line crossed where spiritual calling gave way to market opportunity. After a heated debate, the church council passed a resolution limiting the project's budget and scale. Still, the project moved forward in a scaled-down

---

[8] Wayne A. Meeks, *The Economic World of Early Christianity* (Yale University Press, 1989) Chapter 2: Meeks explores the economic world of the early Christian communities, arguing that they functioned as an alternative economic system to the Roman Empire. Meeks draws on a range of sources, including New Testament texts, non-canonical writings, and archaeological evidence.

form. Then, not long afterward, one of the most outspoken opposing elders was abruptly suspended from leadership for one year. No official reason was given. But many within the church suspected it was retaliation for his dissent.

That moment stayed with me.

I began to reflect more deeply on the relationship between money and ministry, between loyalty and leverage. And I recalled a sermon I had once preached on Acts 4 and 5, on the contrast between Barnabas, and the couple Ananias and Sapphira. Barnabas had sold his field and laid the entire proceeds at the apostles' feet, with no agenda. No performance. Just genuine surrender. But Ananias and Sapphira also sold a piece of property. What made their story tragic was not the amount they gave, but the lie they told. They wanted to appear faithful without the cost of actual sacrifice. They wanted recognition without full surrender.[9]

What struck me then, and what strikes me now, is how subtle that deception can be. When giving becomes performance, when loyalty is coerced or traded for position, when generosity is leveraged for influence, something sacred is lost. Barnabas's gift built the church. Ananias and Sapphira's gift threatened it.

The more I served in this church, the more I saw that same danger lurking beneath the surface, not necessarily in individual hearts, but in the system itself. Money flowed in and out of the church with incredible velocity. Large sums were spent on equipment, events, media, and even meals. On one hand, the generosity was real, many members gave sincerely. On the other hand, there was a silent

---

[9] Matthew Boffey, "5 Insights for Interpreting the Deaths of Ananias and Sapphira" *Logos* (May 2021, https://www.logos.com/grow/5-insights-for-interpreting-the-deaths-of-ananias-and-sapphira/): The article examines the biblical narrative in its historical and cultural context and explores the ethical implications of Ananias and Sapphira's actions.

pressure: to give, to conform, to belong.

The financial relationships created strength, but also silence.

Voices that raised questions were viewed as disloyal. Proposals were rarely evaluated on theological or pastoral grounds alone; their feasibility, budget implications, and optics mattered just as much if not more. And slowly, the soul of ministry began to feel like a department within a corporation.

Of course, the church must operate in the world. Budgets are necessary. Structures are helpful. But when economic entanglements become the glue that holds a congregation together, we must ask: What is the church becoming?

The early church was not just a spiritual community, it was an economic one. But that economy was grounded in trust, transparency, and mutual dependence rooted in Christ. When Ananias and Sapphira lied, they weren't just lying to the apostles, they were lying to the Holy Spirit, violating the sacred trust of the community.

That kind of trust is fragile. And once broken, it's hard to rebuild.

What troubled me most wasn't the presence of money or structure. It was the absence of space to question it. To ask, "Is this truly what God wants?" To wonder if the bond between us was Christ, or contracts.

In many ways, the strength of the church community was beautiful. But it was also unsettling to witness how the circulation of money tightened the web. The more money moved, the more unity was assumed. And yet, I couldn't shake the question:

Were we truly unified in Christ?
Or simply entangled by something else?

Chapter 3
Rituals and Practices

Note 09
Funeral

A few months passed after I resigned from the church. For the first time in over two decades, I was no longer in motion. It was only then that I realized how long I had gone without a real rest without stopping to breathe. For more than twenty years, I had lived as a marketer, businessman, consultant, seminary student, and pastor, often all at once. At first, the sudden stillness unsettled me. But then I began to experience something I hadn't known in years: true rest. I caught up on books I had long shelved, watched movies I had postponed again and again, and finally let myself sleep in. I was grateful for the margin, but also uneasy, haunted by a quiet dread about how long this break would last, and what would come after it.

During that time, I often thought about a friend I had known for many years, someone I had met through my older sister. He had lived with type 1 diabetes since childhood, and for as long as I had known him, he had struggled with a chronic, non-healing wound on his toe. Though we lived far apart, we had kept in touch occasionally. And once I moved to New York, he had only been a short drive away in New Jersey just across the bridge. But ministry had consumed me. Despite his kindness and the warmth with which he always welcomed me, I never managed to visit him. Over time, I heard bits and pieces through others: the wound had worsened, then escalated. Eventually, one of his legs was amputated. Later, I heard of multiple hospitalizations due to complications.

In the fall of 2020, as COVID-19 variants triggered new surges and another round of lockdowns loomed, I got word through an acquaintance: he was now in hospice, nearing the end. And he had asked to see me.

With a heavy heart, I made my way to the hospice. I wasn't sure what to expect. But when I entered the room, I was not prepared for what I saw. He lay in the bed, unrecognizable. Both legs gone. His arms deformed from repeated strokes. His skin grey and paper-thin. His once-sturdy frame had withered into frailty. He looked so fragile, so far from the man I had once known. And in that moment, I was struck by a profound shame: how could I, as a pastor, have gone so long without visiting him? How had I let all those years pass without reaching out, not once, while he suffered, only minutes away?

"Brother, how have you been? I'm sorry it took me so long to find you," I said, unsure of how to speak. But he welcomed me with grace. He told me his story how his body had been gradually ravaged by one complication after another, how he had reached the end of medical intervention, and how he had made peace with what was coming. He had signed the DNR orders. He had stopped all medications. All that remained now was to wait for death. And yet, in that waiting, I saw something remarkable: a calm spirit, anchored by a deep faith. There was no fear in his voice. Only clarity.

Because of COVID restrictions, our time together was limited. But we made the most of it. We prayed. We worshiped. I held his hand. And when I left, I felt something I didn't expect: strange peace.

Two days later, I got another call. He had passed. His family told me he had one final request: that I officiate his funeral.

At first, I froze. This was no ordinary request. His father was a founding elder of the church I had just left, the same church whose leadership had cast me out. Under normal circumstances, the senior pastor of that church would have presided over the service. But the family honored the dying wish of their son. Still, I knew what it meant for me to stand at that pulpit again, even if not within those walls. The tension with my former church was unresolved. The discomfort was real. But after seeing my friend one last time, I knew I could not refuse. I owed him at least that much.

The funeral was small, restricted by pandemic guidelines. We gathered in a subdued room with spaced chairs and masked mourners. In the service, I shared one of my favorite verses: John 8:32, "Then you will know the truth, and the truth will set you free." It was not a cliché. I had seen that freedom. I had seen it in my friend's face, on his deathbed. No machines. No medication. No fear. Just a quiet, fearless dignity clothed in the truth of Christ. That day, I testified to what I saw: a man free in his final moments, not because of what he had or what he'd overcome, but because of who he had trusted.

That funeral became the last service I ever officiated. As I stepped out of the chapel, I noticed a line of people in the parking lot, those who couldn't enter due to social distancing. And as I walked toward my car, I recognized a few faces former church members and staff from the congregation I had left. Our greetings were polite, but awkward. The air was thick with everything we didn't say.

Driving home, I couldn't shake the guilt. I had waited until the very end to see him. Even with every excuse in the world such as ministry demands, distance, and pandemic, I had still failed to love him well. I should have been there. Long before he asked. And yet, another part of me felt quietly angry, not just with myself, but with all of us. Every person at that funeral had loved him. But how many had reached out while he was still alive?

It was his voice that found me.

Not the other way around.
It took his death to bring us together.

Even now, I wonder: Do we truly love people the way we claim to in our prayers? Do we only honor their pain once it's too late? I left the funeral feeling both grateful and ashamed, grateful for the grace I had received in seeing him once more, and ashamed for the pastor I had been. I had served in ministry for more than ten years. But that day, I didn't feel like a shepherd. I felt like a bystander late, silent, and guilty.

And that feeling hasn't left me since.

Note 10
Marriage

Few things in life bring more joy than the conception of a child between two people who love each other. Psalm 127:3 says, "Behold, children are a heritage from the Lord, the fruit of the womb a reward." In most Christian communities, this truth is upheld with reverence and gratitude. Children are viewed as divine gifts and signs of blessing.[10] But this blessing, as it's traditionally understood in the church, is only celebrated when it occurs within the institutional structure of marriage. Sexual intimacy outside of marriage, as clearly outlined in Genesis 2:23, Matthew 19:5, and 1 Corinthians 6:18, is deemed sinful and a violation of biblical order.

While serving as a pastor to a young adult ministry, I encountered a situation that deeply challenged how we, as a church, interpret and apply these teachings. It involved a couple I had been counseling for quite some time. Like many young couples, they had their ups and downs, and passionate affection followed by conflict, reconciliation followed by another fallout. There were seasons where they seemed inseparable, and others where they couldn't stand to be in the same room. After several cycles of conflict and reconciliation, they eventually reached what seemed like a final decision: to end their relationship for good.

The breakup wasn't easy. Because they belonged to the same church community, there was concern over how their separation might affect others. Would one leave the church? Would they both?

---

[10] Stanley J. Grenz & Roger E. Olson, *20th century theology: God and the world in a transitional age* (InterVarsity Press, 1992, Downers Grove, IL): Chapter 8: The author provides insights into the role of children and their significance in the Christian community.

How would they continue worshiping in the same space without causing discomfort for themselves and others? These were not trivial concerns, and out of respect for their shared community, the couple committed to handling the situation with maturity. We spent hours in pastoral counseling working through forgiveness, grief, and release. Eventually, they arrived at a place of peace, a painful but respectful parting, designed to minimize harm both to themselves and to the community.

Then one day, the sister came to see me again, this time alone. She had just discovered that she was pregnant.

What had been closure quickly became a reopening of everything. She was overwhelmed and afraid, unsure of what to do. Suddenly, our counseling wasn't about letting go, but about what came next.

In time, the brother rejoined the conversation. Surprisingly and gratefully, they both came to the same conclusion: they would keep the child, and they would choose to marry. The pregnancy, though unplanned, became a turning point. It pushed them to move beyond the old arguments, beyond the cycles of frustration, and to face the reality of their bond with new humility. I saw in them not a forced obligation, but a mature decision to love more deeply. They decided to recommit, not because they were being told to, but because they wanted to take responsibility for the life they had created and the love they still shared. For me, it was one of the most moving transformations I had witnessed in my pastoral ministry.

Naturally, they wanted to be married in the church, surrounded by the people who had walked with them through their journey. But that request was not warmly received. The church leadership viewed the situation as a violation of purity, a dangerous precedent that could undermine the moral standard expected of members, especially in the young adult community. I was accused of failing to educate and supervise them properly. Discussions among leadership quickly moved from pastoral care to damage control. The couple's desire to set a wedding date and receive pre-marital counseling was put on hold. They were told their situation did not qualify as a priority.

Instead, they were asked to apologize.
To the senior pastor.
To the church council.
And, symbolically, to the congregation at large.

I was tasked with guiding them through the apology process, which felt less like restoration and more like penance. Only after formal repentance was offered were they granted permission to marry in the church building. Even then, the ceremony was marked not by celebration but by a somber tone as if forgiveness had been granted, but joy withheld.

This experience stayed with me. As pastors, we are called to uphold the biblical call to purity. We teach that sex outside of marriage is not God's design. But we are also called to minister with compassion, recognizing that we all fall short in many ways. This couple did not deny their mistake. They did not rebel or justify it. They humbled themselves, took responsibility, and responded with maturity and faith. Yet at the moment when they should have been most supported when they were courageously choosing life and love, they were met not with celebration but with shame.[11]

---

[11] David Kinnaman & Gabe Lyon, *You Lost Me: Why Young Christians Are Leaving Church ... and Rethinking Faith* (Bakers Book, 2016) Chapter 6: The authors discuss how some young adults leave the church because they perceive the church's values as rigid and unchanging, particularly when it comes to issues related to sexuality and gender. The authors argue that

John 8 tells the story of a woman caught in adultery. The law said she should be stoned. The religious leaders dragged her into public to humiliate her, to expose her shame. But Jesus bent down and wrote in the dirt. He said, "Let the one who is without sin cast the first stone." And one by one, the stones dropped. Jesus, the only one who could have condemned her, instead said, "Neither do I condemn you. Go, and sin no more."

Why did Jesus send the woman away without interrogating her about her sin without demanding an explanation, a confession, or public repentance?

In Genesis 3:10, when Adam hears the voice of God in the garden, he hides. "I was afraid because I was naked," he says.

The first consequence of sin was not punishment, but shame.

It is shame, not guilt that drives us to cover ourselves, to retreat from others, to hide from God. And the deeper deceit of sin is that it doesn't just bring shame, it teaches us to conceal it. It convinces us that hiding is safer than healing, that secrecy is more righteous than exposure.

The woman's shame was already public. According to the law, she should have been stoned or at the very least, humiliated. But Jesus, seeing that her sin was already laid bare, refused to humiliate her further. He saw her shame, and rather than weaponizing it, He absorbed it. That's what He would do again on the cross.

---

many young adults want the church to be more open to discussion and dialogue about these issues and to approach them with greater nuance and empathy. When the church appears to be imposing its values on young people in a one-sided manner, many young adults feel alienated and disconnected from the church. The authors suggest that the church needs to find ways to engage with young people in a more open and flexible manner, allowing for a diversity of perspectives and experiences.

As Isaiah 50:6 says, "I gave my back to those who strike me, and my cheeks to those who pull out the beard; I did not hide my face from insult and spitting." Jesus didn't come to shame sinners. He came to bear the shame that sin brings. He did not expose our wounds, He let Himself be wounded instead.

That's why I struggled when I witnessed the church leadership demanding a public confession, ritual apology, and symbolic humiliation from a couple whose shame had already been exposed. Is it really restoration if it reopens wounds that grace has already covered?

> *Wouldn't Jesus have looked at that couple and simply said:*
> *"You've made the hard choice.*
> *Now go, love one another.*
> *Raise your child with tenderness.*
> *And do not be afraid."*

Note 11
Appointment

In Acts 6, the early church in Jerusalem faced a crisis. Growth had brought tension. The apostles, recognizing their limits, delegated responsibility. They instructed the community to appoint seven men who were "known to be full of the Spirit and wisdom" to oversee the daily distribution of food. This was the foundation for what many churches today understand as the diaconate and the broader principle of shared leadership. That scriptural model, spiritual maturity, and godly character, remains the ideal standard. And yet, as I discovered while serving in church administration, reality often looks very different.

One of the most memorable experiences I had while serving in the administrative staff of this particular church was overseeing the appointment of new deacons and elders. Given the size of the church, it was logistically impossible to assess the personal spiritual depth of every member. So we relied on measurable indicators such as worship attendance, giving records, volunteer involvement, and class participation. Those who met or exceeded the threshold were added to the nomination pool. From there, the congregation would vote to select a set number of candidates.

The election itself, in this particular case, went smoothly. Nominations, voting, and counting were handled with integrity. There were no disputes. Once the results were finalized, the new officers entered a months-long period of training and preparation. The installation ceremony was massive, hundreds of people being ordained in one coordinated event. It was orderly, dignified, and celebrated with genuine joy.

The process was complex, but it functioned well. It minimized subjective bias, offered a sense of transparency, and, for the most part, resulted in the appointment of dedicated and competent leaders. In the months that followed, most of the new officers served the church faithfully.

Towards the end of the year, the staff and council held a joint retreat to develop a vision and strategic plan for the upcoming year of ministry. All newly appointed elders were in attendance, and discussions focused on each department's goals and direction. A summary presentation was shared during the retreat, which included the proposed vision for the new church building then under construction. During that presentation, the senior pastor brought up the anticipated construction costs, and directly asked the new elders to contribute a specific amount toward the expense.

It remains unclear whether the requested contributions were actually made, or how the nature of the offering was officially defined. Was it a "thanksgiving offering" for their ordination? Or a designated "building fund" donation? Either way, what is clear is that the newly appointed elders were explicitly singled out and asked to give a set amount. There was nothing subtle about it. The senior pastor made the demand explicitly and firmly, leaving little room for ambiguity. The newly appointed elders weren't just encouraged, they were directly instructed to contribute a specific amount.

And that's when the word returned to me: Simony.

Simony is the practice of buying or selling spiritual privileges, church offices, sacraments, or blessings. The word comes from Simon the sorcerer in Acts 8, who tried to purchase the power of the Holy Spirit from the apostles. In church history, simony was rampant, especially in the 11th century. Wealthy individuals paid for positions of power, and clergy exchanged spiritual authority for material gain. It was a corruption so severe that it helped fuel the Protestant Reformation. It wasn't until the Council of Trent in the 16th century that the church formally condemned the practice as a crime.[12]

Of course, in modern churches, no one "sells" titles outright. But that doesn't mean the temptation is gone. When expectations of financial giving are quietly attached to leadership roles, even informally we risk drifting into the same ethical failure. When people feel they must "show gratitude" with money to secure their place, or when leadership becomes tied to status and social capital, something of the gospel is lost.

To be clear, the election itself had been conducted with fairness.
The criteria were consistent.
The training was thoughtful.
But the financial expectation, unstated yet, unmistakable undermined everything that came before it.

The New Testament is explicit about the qualifications for church leaders. Acts 6, 1 Timothy, 2 Timothy, and Titus all emphasize spiritual maturity, good reputation, sound doctrine, and servant-heartedness.

There is no mention of wealth.
No emphasis on contribution.

---

[12] Eamon Duffy, *The Voices of Morebath: Reformation and rebellion in an English village* (Yale University Press, 1997) Chapter 4, 5: The Council of Trent was a significant event in the history of the Catholic Church, which took place in Trento, Italy, from 1545 to 1563. It was convened by Pope Paul III to address the challenges posed by the Protestant Reformation and to reform and strengthen the Catholic Church. During the Council of Trent, important issues were debated and decided upon, including the interpretation of Scripture, the role of tradition in the Church, the nature of the sacraments, and the importance of the priesthood. The council also addressed the issue of simony, which had become widespread in the Church at the time. It declared that simony was a grave sin and imposed severe penalties on those who engaged in it.

And certainly no room for financial obligation tied to ordination.

In this case, what should have been a moment of sacred commissioning carried a hidden cost.

The church must guard against such distortions.
The danger is subtle.
It rarely looks like corruption on the surface.
It often wears the language of "honor" or "gratitude."

But when leadership is associated even loosely, with money, influence, or expectation, the spiritual integrity of the church is at stake.

We must return to the model of Acts: Spirit-filled people, chosen for wisdom, appointed in prayer, and released to serve, not because they gave enough, but because they had been called.

Anything less may appear functional.
But it isn't faithful.

Note 12
Pastoral Visit

In large congregations, it's often difficult for a pastor to know the life situation of every member. That's why many churches divide the congregation into parishes and assign a parish pastor or evangelist to each group, creating a system of care and connection. Within this system, pastoral visits meeting with families in their homes for prayer, conversation, and sometimes worship, are considered an important part of spiritual care.

During my time at the church I eventually resigned from, I was regularly invited to conduct these pastoral visits. Some were for prayer or blessing, others for personal counseling, illness, or family transitions. Shortly after my installation, I received my first such invitation. The request had come through the parish evangelist, who had selected me from among several associate pastors. The visit was ordinary in every way: warm conversation, a brief time of prayer, and a few encouraging words.

But something unexpected happened on the way back. The evangelist handed me an envelope. When I asked about it, she said it was "a token of appreciation from the family" a long-standing tradition in the church, she added. I was surprised, but I didn't question it too much at the time.

From that moment on, the pattern repeated itself. After most visits, the evangelist would quietly pass along an envelope, usually containing a modest sum. The amount was never fixed, but over time, the extra income became a regular supplement to my salary which, to be honest, was barely enough to support a family in the city.

The invitations varied: some for birthdays, business openings, family crises, or prayers for healing. I told myself it was part of the job. And it was. But gradually, I began to notice something else forming in me: expectation. I didn't want to admit it, but I started anticipating the envelope. I didn't ask for it. I never demanded it. But when it didn't come, I felt something disappointment. That realization shook me.

Jesus taught His disciples to care for the sick, the imprisoned, the stranger. "When you did it for the least of these," He said, "you did it for me" (Matthew 25:40). James wrote that "true religion" is to care for orphans and widows, and to keep oneself unstained by the world (James 1:27). Pastoral care is meant to be a reflection of those values rooted in compassion, selflessness, and presence.

And to be fair, the visits did bear fruit. They created bonds between pastors and families. They opened doors to spiritual conversations that would never happen on a Sunday. They allowed me to understand people's lives in a way that no sermon ever could. And the modest gifts helped pastors stay afloat in a difficult economy.

But therein lies the subtle danger.

When care becomes tied to compensation, when spiritual presence becomes predictably rewarded, we are no longer simply shepherds. We are spiritual service providers. And I began to fear that the quality and quantity of care might eventually depend, not on spiritual discernment or need, but on the economic capacity of the household. I don't mean to project this onto all pastors. I can only speak for myself. But I know how easily good intentions can drift. And I know how difficult it is to untangle ourselves once that drift begins to feel normal.

What disturbed me more was how embedded this system was.

No one questioned it. It had been happening for decades. Parish evangelists treated it as routine. Congregants had come to expect it as part of the "pastoral visit package." It wasn't malicious. It wasn't even obviously corrupt. But it was… transactional. And I couldn't shake the feeling that something sacred was being eroded, slowly and quietly.

The history of the church offers painful warnings about this kind of drift. The corruption of the medieval church didn't begin with outright abuse. It began with the blending of spiritual care and monetary expectation. With blurred lines. With unspoken norms. With spiritual authority being packaged, and sometimes sold.

And I saw traces of that in myself.

Then one day, something unexpected happened. I was invited to visit a young man who had been struggling personally and had stopped attending church altogether. He didn't want anything formal, just someone to talk to. When I arrived, he had prepared a simple meal, though he confessed he didn't know how to cook. The rice was undercooked. The soup was too salty. But none of that mattered. He poured out his heart as we sat together. He talked, and I listened. We laughed. We cried. And when words ran out, we prayed.

There was no envelope.
No evangelist coordinating the visit.
No expectation.
Just presence.
Just grace.

In that unpolished, unscripted moment, I remembered what ministry felt like before the systems, before the calculations, before the rewards.

And I realized: this: this quiet, broken, honest encounter, was the very heart of pastoral ministry.

Chapter 4
Beyond the Church Walls

Note 13
Forsaken

The reality of resigning from pastoral ministry was far more brutal than I had anticipated. For over a decade, my phone had never been quiet: text messages, calls, prayer requests, last-minute pastoral needs, meetings, event reminders, and small encouragements came almost every hour of the day. But after I left, it all stopped. Overnight. The silence was immediate and complete, as if someone had cut the power and all the bright lights, colors, and noise that once surrounded me disappeared. At first, I was stunned. Then I felt disoriented. And before long, the silence became suffocating.

That silence wasn't just the absence of noise. It was the absence of people, people I had prayed with, cried with, led in worship, visited in hospitals, and counseled through some of the hardest moments of their lives. In a single moment, I had become invisible to them. Forgotten, or perhaps deliberately avoided. I wasn't even sure which was worse.

Then one day, my wife received a call from a member of our former church. Her voice trembled as she spoke.

"I don't know exactly what your husband did," she said, *"but whatever it was, it's not right for the senior pastor to speak about him like that during a sermon this morning. I still believe in your husband. I still support him."*

Curious and concerned, my wife searched online and found the sermon. It had been live-streamed and was archived on the church's

YouTube channel. She watched it alone. I didn't have the heart to watch it with her, or to watch it at all. But when she began to sob uncontrollably, I knew enough. Her tears said everything. Whatever had been said from the pulpit wasn't just unkind, it was condemning. I hadn't even been gone long, and already my name had become a lesson in failure.

In time, a few members tried to reach out again, but I couldn't bring myself to answer. The senior pastor had warned me explicitly not to contact any members after my resignation. And frankly, I didn't have the emotional energy to rekindle relationships. Even the smallest attempt at reconnection felt like trying to breathe underwater. So instead, I turned inward. I read. I listened to music. I kept my hands busy. I filled the silence with distractions.

But despite everything I did to occupy myself, there was still a void I couldn't ignore.

As days turned to weeks, and weeks to months, I began to return to the Scriptures. Not as a teacher or preacher, but simply as a reader. A wounded reader, seeking something to hold on to. I slowed down. I wrote notes in the margins. I prayed more simply, and more honestly. Somewhere in that quiet return to the Word, the void began to fill, not quickly, but gently. And it was then that I began to recognize something I hadn't wanted to name: **the feeling of being forsaken.**

It wasn't just disappointment. It wasn't even just grief. It was deeper. It was the aching, unspoken knowledge that I had been severed from the very community I had once helped shepherd. I felt like a man cast away on a deserted island. I hadn't committed a crime. I hadn't harmed anyone. But I had vanished from the lives of people who once embraced me, and it felt like exile.

What gave me peace, strangely, was the sense that I had not been forsaken by God. I clung to that truth. But the news still came to me, every so often, like poison dropped into water that the senior pastor continued to mention me from the pulpit, continued to frame my departure in ways I couldn't respond to. I didn't fight back. I stayed silent. But each word spoken in my absence felt like another layer of weight pressing down on me. Silence, at times, is strength. But in those days, it felt like surrender.

A pastor friend of mine continued to check in on me after I left. He was kind, careful, and loyal. But eventually, even he was rebuked by the senior pastor publicly, during a staff meeting for continuing to maintain contact with me. A few months later, he resigned too.

Still, I said nothing. Instead, I dug deeper into the Word. I asked questions I had never allowed myself to ask:

"What is God's will in all of this?"
"Why does abandonment hurt more than opposition?"
"Where is Christ in this silence?"

Then one day, Isaiah 53 found me. "He was despised and rejected by men; a man of sorrows, acquainted with grief; like one from whom men hide their faces, He was despised, and we esteemed Him not."

That verse broke something in me. It wasn't just that Jesus understood the pain of rejection. It was that I had begun this journey hoping He would identify with my suffering, but suddenly, I realized I was the one who had rejected Him. The betrayal He experienced wasn't just historical, it was personal. My personal. He had been spat upon, mocked, deserted, crucified, not just by strangers, but by those closest to Him. The same crowd that waved palm branches turned against Him in less than a week. The same disciples who swore loyalty denied even knowing Him. And in that moment, I saw that I, too, had stood among the crowd. I, too, had denied Him, not with words, but with silence, with compromise, with politics, with performance dressed in holiness.

I remembered all the moments I had tolerated injustice to preserve peace. All the times I had nodded in meetings when I should have spoken up. All the decisions I had made that prioritized order over righteousness. All the ways I had protected my position at the cost of His name. I thought I had been cast out. But in truth, I had cast Him out again and again.

The deeper I went into Scripture, the more clearly I saw:
I hadn't just been forsaken.
I had been a forsaker.

And yet, He did not abandon me. The wound of being forsaken turned into something else. It stopped being about the pain others had caused me, and started becoming a path, a path of repentance, of honesty, of redefinition. My prayers changed. I no longer cried out, "Lord, why was I rejected?" I began asking, "Lord, where are You leading me next?"

In the silence, I began to walk again.
Not toward restoration of my former role.
Not toward vindication.
But toward Jesus.
And that was enough.

Note 14
Revealed

Leaving ministry didn't just mark the end of a chapter. It uncovered things I had avoided looking at for a long time. The first thing it revealed was myself.

I used to believe I was someone who served God with sincerity. And in many ways, I had. But along the way, I also found myself caught between competing forces: between church leadership and congregation, between what I understood as biblical conviction and what was institutionally expected of me. In that tension, I often compromised, sometimes quietly, sometimes openly. I justified it as necessary for ministry, or for unity, or for survival. But the truth is, there were moments when I gave in, even though I knew deep down it wasn't what God wanted.

One of those compromises still lingers with me: the sheer number of church events we produced, and how much energy was spent keeping people constantly occupied. At one point, I heard someone say, "The church is healthiest when people are too busy to think." That line stuck with me. Not because I agreed, but because I had seen how that mentality shaped everything we did.

The church calendar was packed year-round with programs, meetings, and large-scale events. Every department was mobilized. Every volunteer was stretched. Staff members worked late into the night, not because they were lazy or inefficient, but because the system never stopped moving. People sacrificed weekends, family time, and even their health, often without knowing exactly why. There was little room to rest, much less to reflect.

Over time, it became clear that simply keeping the system running was treated as a measure of spiritual health. If someone burned out, it was quietly suggested that they lacked faith. If someone questioned the need for another event, they were seen as uncooperative. That kind of pressure was rarely spoken, but it was deeply felt. Looking back, I wonder how often I contributed to it.

What did all that activity actually produce? There were successful events, full rooms, generous offerings, and sometimes local media coverage. But when I thought about how little time we actually spent focusing on the Lord in the process, it left me unsettled. We were always busy doing things "for God," but rarely pausing to ask whether He had asked for them.

That question reminded me of a passage in Mark 9. The disciples see someone casting out demons in Jesus' name and try to stop him. He wasn't part of their group, and they didn't like that. But Jesus says, "Don't stop him. No one who does a mighty work in my name will soon after speak evil of me. Whoever is not against us is for us." What struck me wasn't just the rebuke, it was the contrast in perspective. The disciples were focused on who was in and who was out. Jesus was focused on whose name was being honored. For the disciples, ministry had become something to protect. For Jesus, it was something to give away freely.

That helped me see myself more clearly.

Over time, I found myself thinking that quality ministry required scale, polish, and precision. I don't think I ever fully believed that in my heart, but the constant pace of events, the pressure to produce, and the unspoken standards of success within the church made it feel that way. It became easy to assume that bigger was better, and that excellence could be measured by attendance, budget, or visibility. But when I returned to the Gospels, I was reminded that Jesus pointed to something much simpler: His name. His presence. His work carried out by people who weren't trying to impress anyone, just trying to be faithful.

I had a chance to test that conviction during a young adult event we were planning. In the past, events like this were closely managed by staff pastors and elders. The common assumption was that only experienced leaders could ensure the event would meet the church's standards. But this time, I proposed something different: to give full responsibility to the young adults themselves. I believed it would be more meaningful if they planned, prayed, and led the event on their own, even if it didn't look perfect.

The idea was met with resistance. Some of the leadership felt it was too risky, too informal, or too small in scale. There were suggestions to bring in guest speakers, invite other churches, and make it a larger regional event. I disagreed, and after a series of difficult conversations, I was finally able to persuade the senior pastor to allow it. With that approval, I stepped back and let the young adults take full ownership. I stayed involved only to encourage and pray for them along the way.

What happened wasn't perfect. But it was honest.

They met regularly, prayed together, and encouraged one another. They invited friends. They worked through conflicts. And when the day of the event came, it wasn't flashy, but it was full of heart. I could tell, just by being in the room, that something real was happening. For many of them, it was the first time they had taken spiritual ownership of anything. For some, it was the reason they came back to church. For others, it was the moment they realized their faith was still alive.

It reminded me that ministry doesn't have to be impressive to be meaningful. It just has to be true.

People often tell us to think big in ministry. Reach more. Make it excellent. Make it visible. But in Mark 9:41, Jesus says, "If anyone gives you even a cup of water because you belong to Christ, they will certainly not lose their reward."

That verse doesn't condemn ambition. But it does shift the focus.

These days, I think more often about the small things. A thoughtful prayer. A quiet conversation. A few young people deciding, on their own, to do something for the Lord, not because they were told to, but because they wanted to. These aren't things that make headlines. But they're not small to Him.

And that's enough for me.

Note 15
Enlighten

For as long as I can remember, the Lord's Day never felt restful. In fact, it often felt like a battle. I know I'm not the only one who felt that way. Many pastors and churchgoers alike have come to associate Sunday with nonstop activity, obligation, and exhaustion. For years, I lived that rhythm without questioning it. Even though the Scriptures speak of the Sabbath as a day of rest: for your family, your servants, even your animals, it was never truly rest for me. Sunday was the busiest, most demanding day of the week.

After stepping away from the church, that changed. At first, it was just my wife and me. We would rise early on Sundays and prepare a simple time of worship. We shared the Word, reflected quietly, and prayed. Then we rested. There were no lights to turn on, no service outlines to finalize, no classrooms to check, no rehearsals or last-minute printouts. We didn't end the day physically and emotionally drained. We ended it grateful and rested.

A while later, that quiet rhythm began to grow. A few others expressed interest in joining us. These days, we worship together as a small house church. It's just a few families, gathering simply, sometimes in person, sometimes online. There's no name, no signage, no brand. Just a shared desire to seek the Lord. The services are brief, the prayers sincere, and the time together is unhurried. There are no programs to run, no deadlines to meet. And for the first time in years, the Lord's Day feels like what it was meant to be: restful and full of grace. There are also a few people who, though unable to join us in person, have asked to receive the recorded sermon files each week. So I record and send it along. Quietly, without much fuss, it has become a way to remain connected, and to keep the Word going out.

That realization led me to reflect on how Sunday had become so far removed from its purpose. I wasn't the only one who had carried that weight. I had seen countless volunteers: nursery workers, ushers, choir members, and kitchen teams, serve for hours on end, barely catching a break. Some of them were energized by it, and I don't want to dismiss the joy that comes from serving. But the question still lingers: how did a day that was meant to be a gift of rest turn into the busiest, most exhausting day of the week?

The answer, I think, lies deeper than just church culture. It goes back to something more foundational, something introduced at the very beginning.

In Genesis 3, the serpent tells the woman, "If you eat of it, your eyes will be opened, and you will be like God, knowing good and evil." That phrase knowing good and evil, has been the subject of countless theological discussions. But at its core, it introduces something foreign to Eden: human comparison. Judgment. Measurement.

Before the fruit, Adam and Eve were naked, and they felt no shame. But after they ate, they covered themselves, not because anything had changed externally, but because their perception had changed. They now had a standard. And with that standard came shame. Good vs. bad. Valuable vs. worthless. Beautiful vs. ugly. Ever since that moment, humanity has lived under the weight of this framework, constantly striving, comparing, proving.

That same framework has shaped how we approach even holy things. We measure Sunday not by rest or reflection, but by attendance numbers, service length, the size of the offering, or how smoothly everything ran. We evaluate our worship by volume, our fellowship by turnout, our service by the number of tasks completed. Somewhere along the way, even the Lord's Day became something we had to manage and prove ourselves through.

But Eden was never about productivity. It wasn't a place of performance. It was a place of presence of walking with God in the cool of the day. It was a space created not for striving, but for dwelling. Not for proving, but for trusting. Many theological traditions have framed the tree of the knowledge of good and evil as a test of obedience, an opportunity for humans to exercise free will. But what if that tree wasn't placed there simply as a test? What if it was there because it, too, reflected something of God Himself?

When we look closely at Genesis 2, Eden is more than a garden. It's a reflection of God's very nature. The river flowing from its center points to God as the source of life.[13] The command for Adam to cultivate and keep the garden mirrors God's role as sovereign and caretaker. Naming the animals speaks to God's authority and relational design. The union of man and woman reflects God's communal being. The tree of life reveals His eternal nature.

In that context, the tree of the knowledge of good and evil wasn't a divine trap, it was another aspect of God's character. After all, the ability to discern good from evil is part of God's wisdom and sovereignty.[14] That tree stood in Eden because nothing of God's essence was withheld from the world He created. Eden was not a test site, it was a visible reflection of an invisible God. And everything in it,

---

[13] In Revelation 22:1-2, it describes the New Jerusalem as a garden with a river of life flowing through it, similar to the garden of Eden. This suggests that the garden of Eden may have been a prototype for the ultimate paradise that awaits believers in the end times.
[14] Victor P. Hamilton, *The book of Genesis: Chapters 1-17, Vol. 1* (Wm. B. Eerdmans Publishing., 1990): 116-118: The author argues that this knowledge was originally the exclusive domain of God, and that Adam and Eve's disobedience in eating from the tree of the knowledge of good and evil was a usurpation of divine prerogative.

including that tree, revealed something true about Him.

The tragedy came when the serpent twisted that reflection. He convinced humans to reach for what wasn't theirs to possess. The temptation wasn't just about disobedience, it was about adopting a standard that didn't belong to them. The moment they ate the fruit, Adam and Eve saw themselves, and everything around them differently. Not through God's eyes, but through the lens of comparison and shame. They were already made in God's image. But now, they lived by a new metric: one that measured value, status, and worth by human judgment

And that shift replacing God's presence with human standards, is still with us today.

The tragedy wasn't just that humanity disobeyed. It's that we took what belonged to God alone, the right to define good and evil, and used it to redefine ourselves. And ever since, we've been using that standard to measure everything including worship.

That realization made me take another look at how we had been living out the Lord's Day. Was our version of Sunday truly honoring God? Or were we honoring our own standards of success? Did our full calendars reflect His presence, or just our planning? Did we gather to rest with Him, or to prove ourselves useful?

These days, my Sundays are slower. There's less movement, but more meaning. I don't preach from a stage. I sit around a table. I don't strive to impress. I simply try to be present with God, and with others.

There's no production, no pressure.
Just a few families, a shared meal, an open Bible, and rest.
And somehow, that has been enough.

*Maybe that's what the Lord intended all along.
Not for us to exhaust ourselves in His name,
but to remember that even resting with Him is an act of worship.*

Note 16
Forsaking

I once attended the retirement ceremony of a senior pastor I had long respected. During his final reflection, he said something that struck a deep chord: "Because I was a pastor, sometimes I couldn't get closer to people I wanted to know better, and I couldn't keep distance from people I was uncomfortable around. I was always surrounded by others, but I was rarely known. Looking back, I realize that ministry has been a very lonely journey." I remember nodding quietly as he spoke, feeling as though he had put words to something I had never fully admitted to myself.

Even when I wanted genuine fellowship within the church, I often held back. I feared misunderstanding, jealousy, or criticism. There were many times I couldn't say no to members I found deeply challenging, and even when I was emotionally drained or personally struggling, I had to stay available. I never quite had the space to be a person first, but only a pastor.

This wasn't just true of relationships. It was true of worship. Every Sunday, I put on the expected demeanor. I stood behind the pulpit and presented my "best self" whether or not I was doing well. Whether I had argued with my wife that morning, or felt angry, afraid, or numb, I led the congregation as though everything in me was steady and whole. That wasn't hypocrisy, it was survival.

What I see more clearly now is that the structure of church, the formality, the liturgy, the rhythm of songs and prayers, can provide a kind of shield. The very atmosphere of holiness can become a refuge for hiding. The order of service, the ritual of standing and sitting, the shared creeds and confessions, all of it can create a space where no one has to confront what they're really carrying. It can become a place where even pastors can hide behind sacred language and never name what's truly happening in their hearts.

And the Scriptures knew this. That's why verses like these carry so much weight:
"To obey is better than sacrifice" (1 Samuel 15:22).
"I desire steadfast love and not sacrifice" (Hosea 6:6).
"To do righteousness and justice is more acceptable to the Lord than sacrifice" (Proverbs 21:3).

God never dismissed worship. But He warned us not to confuse it with performance. He cares more about the posture of the heart than the perfection of the service. He wants worshipers who walk with Him, not just those who appear to be faithful on Sunday.

After I left the church, I found myself feeling exposed in a way I hadn't expected. Without a congregation, without a pulpit, without the structure of church life around me, I began to feel like I was wandering in unfamiliar terrain. There was no bulletin to follow, no community to lean on, no church identity to cover me. For the first time in years, I was standing outside of the protective structure that had, in many ways, shaped how I saw myself. And in that open space, I began to feel a different kind of pressure. Not the pressure to perform, but the pressure of not knowing who I was anymore.

What does a pastor look like when no one's watching?
Where is the ministry when there's no church building, no program, no title?
Had I become dependent on the structure, the atmosphere, even the reverence of the sanctuary to feel close to God?

I prayed more honestly than I had in a long time. And slowly, the Lord began to speak, not in the formal ways I was used to, but in quiet impressions, in tears, in silence. He reminded me that He searches the heart, not the title (Proverbs 16:2). That what matters most is not how things appear, but what's true when everything else is stripped away.

"I appeal to you, brothers, by the mercies of God, to present your bodies as a living sacrifice, holy and acceptable to God which is your spiritual worship." (Romans 12:1)

That verse meant something new now. I realized how often I had given "partial sacrifices" good sermons, faithful programs, public prayers, all while hiding unresolved parts of myself. But when I found myself worshiping in silence, with no one to impress, no stage to stand on, and no expectations to meet, I discovered a new kind of worship.

Sometimes I confessed my sadness.
Sometimes I wept in anger.
Sometimes I sat in silence, ashamed of my weakness.

But that worship unfiltered, honest, and vulnerable, became the most holy I had ever known. There was no stained glass. No worship team. No applause. Just me. And God. And that was enough. Letting go of the layers such as my role, my image, and my performance, wasn't easy. But once I did, I discovered something far better.

Worship, finally, became worship.

Unshackled: *A Story Unfolding Beyond the Church Walls*

Chapter 5
Unshackled

Note 17
To the Ends of the Earth

Around the turn of the millennium, a new missionary movement emerged, rooted in a renewed urgency to fulfill the Great Commission. The goal was clear: reach the 10,000+ unreached people groups around the world those who had never heard the name of Jesus. Churches, mission organizations, and training centers poured resources into the task. Strategies were developed. Regions were mapped. And a new generation of missionaries was sent out, committed to taking the gospel "to the ends of the earth."[15]

Among my long-time acquaintances was a missionary couple who devoted many years to a minority group in rural China. They learned the language, built trust with the local people, translated Scripture and hymns, and quietly shared the gospel. Eventually, the husband passed away due to illness after years of labor in obscurity. Their story was not widely known. There were no headlines, no dramatic testimonies. But they embodied the spirit of Acts 1:8.

> "You will receive power when the Holy Spirit comes upon you, and you will be my witnesses in Jerusalem, and in all Judea and Samaria, and to the ends of the earth."

That verse was everywhere during those years plastered on posters, spoken from pulpits, engraved into missions conferences. But

---

[15] Luis Bush, "A Brief Historical Overview of the AD2000 & Beyond Movement and Joshua Project 2000" *Luisbush Papers* (May 1996, https://luisbushpapers.com/joshua-project/1995/11/01/a-brief-historical-overview-of-the-ad2000-movement-and-joshua-project-2000/)

despite how often I quoted or heard it, I don't think I ever really asked myself what the "ends of the earth" meant for me personally. It was always elsewhere, always someone else's calling. I was busy with ministry inside the church: worship services, programs, staff meetings, and seasonal events. There was always something to prepare, to plan, to lead.

And the church was growing. New families joined regularly. But many of them came from other churches. We celebrated numbers, but if I was honest, we weren't seeing conversions. We weren't reaching the lost. We were redistributing the faithful. Everything we did, we did well, but almost everything we did was for people already within the walls.

At some point, I began to feel a growing discomfort. Where was our witness to those outside? What about the people who had never stepped inside a sanctuary? We preached the gospel, but mostly to one another. And I began to wonder, where is my "end of the earth"? Is it a remote jungle or an urban alley? Is it measured in miles, or in courage? These questions took deeper root after I left church ministry. With the noise gone, I could finally hear them clearly. They unsettled me, not in a guilt-driven way, but in a clarifying way. I wasn't looking to travel far or make a statement. I just wanted to follow where the Spirit led.

That's when I revisited the story of Philip.

Philip wasn't one of the apostles. He was a deacon, tasked with serving the practical needs of the Jerusalem church. But after Stephen's martyrdom and the persecution that followed, believers scattered. Philip went to Samaria. A place long held in contempt by the Jews. But Philip didn't hesitate. He preached Christ there. He healed the sick. He baptized believers. And the city was filled with joy.

The church was thriving. It was a moment of revival, and Philip was right in the center of it. Then came the interruption.

"Rise and go toward the south to the road that goes down from Jerusalem to Gaza. This is a desert place."

The wilderness. Empty. Quiet. A step away from momentum and revival. The text doesn't tell us how Philip felt, but I can imagine. He had just left the bustle of Jerusalem. Now Samaria was bearing fruit. And suddenly, this detour? But Philip obeyed.

That one act of obedience led to a chariot. And inside the chariot was a man from Ethiopia. A royal official. A seeker. Reading Isaiah, but not understanding. Wondering aloud what it all meant. And the Spirit said again, "Go." So Philip ran.

That moment became a hinge in history. The gospel reached a man who would carry it back to his homeland. Scholars believe Ethiopia was among the first nations to embrace Christianity. But none of it looked impressive when it began. It was just a man, a desert road, a question, and a willing heart.

That's how the kingdom moves. Not in flashy stages or explosive campaigns, but in quiet wilderness encounters.

I used to believe that ministry had to be big to be faithful. I thought scale meant success, that impact was visible and measurable. But Philip's story challenged that. He left revival to follow a whisper. He walked into obscurity. He had no guarantees, just a command and a direction. And he ran.

When I think back on my own ministry years, I see so many good things. Faithful people. Deep friendships. Sincere worship. But I also see a system that sometimes mistook activity for obedience, and growth for faithfulness. We programmed our way into momentum, but we often forgot to listen.

What would it look like to follow the Spirit like Philip did? Not just to plan, but to pause? Not just to gather, but to go? The "ends of the earth" may not be a place you can pinpoint on a map. Sometimes, it's the next difficult conversation. Sometimes, it's the marginalized neighbor. Sometimes, it's the part of your city you've always avoided. And sometimes, it's the internal wilderness where you face your own fears and discover that the gospel still holds.

In the Jerusalem model of ministry, you stay. You build. You tend. That's good and holy. But the Spirit also calls us to Samaria, to the people we've overlooked. And then to the desert, where we may find just one soul waiting. I think of the many times I was surrounded by a crowd and felt useful, but disconnected. And I think of the handful of moments when I stepped into something smaller, quieter, unplanned, and found God already there.

Philip's story reminds me that God is always ahead of us, not behind. He's not waiting for us to make church work better. He's inviting us to listen, to follow, to run.

And when I consider what ministry looks like now: fewer people, simpler worship, and fewer expectations, I wonder if perhaps this is my wilderness road. I don't see chariots every day. But I do see people. And I'm learning to listen for the Spirit's whisper again.

The truth is, I still believe in the church. I still believe in community, and worship, and discipleship. But I no longer believe that the kingdom advances by our systems. It moves through surrender. Through those who say yes, even when the road looks empty.

Jesus didn't give Acts 1:8 to just inspire global missions. He gave it to reorient our direction. To remind us that the Spirit's power isn't just for staying, it's for going. From Jerusalem, to Judea and Samaria, and to whatever your wilderness looks like today.

For me, the ends of the earth aren't far away anymore. They're wherever obedience takes me. And I want to be the one who runs.

Note 18
Penniless

After stepping away from the church, I returned to the work I had left behind for ministry. My wife and I resumed marketing consulting together from home, something we had long talked about but never had time to fully pursue. In many ways, it felt like we were recovering lost years, both practically and emotionally. We had lived too long in separate lanes, often divided by the demands of ministry. Now we were sharing daily life again: mornings over coffee, quiet time in the Word, Sunday worship side by side. Though it was just the two of us, our worship felt whole. We didn't need a sanctuary. We didn't need programs. We just needed space to heal and seek the Lord again.

For over a year, that's what we did. We lived simply. We worked, we prayed, we read, we rested. Sunday services were short and sincere, just us, a Bible, a song, and a prayer. That time, stripped of all distractions, brought clarity. We were rediscovering the joy of meeting God in silence, not in spectacle.

Then, in 2022, another family joined us for worship. Just one family. Nothing elaborate changed, and yet everything shifted. A new presence brought new possibilities, and new questions.

Until that point, our worship had been entirely personal: no structure, no schedule, no expectations. But now, I found myself returning to old questions I thought I had buried: What should worship look like? Should we meet weekly? Should we organize tithing? Where do we hold service? What form should preaching take?

It surprised me how quickly these anxieties returned. Though I had walked away from the institutional church, I hadn't fully left its framework behind. I realized that some parts of me were still tethered, especially to the idea that worship had to be managed, structured, and resourced in a certain way. With one more family involved, the weight of "church" began to creep back in, quietly but forcefully.

That's when I revisited the story in John 2, when Jesus went up to Jerusalem for the Passover and drove out the money changers from the temple. The system He confronted was logical. Worshippers traveling from far couldn't bring sacrificial animals, so they bought them at the temple. The temple tax could only be paid in the local shekel, so currency exchange was necessary. On paper, the system made sense.

But in practice, the temple had become a marketplace. Profit and worship had intertwined. Worshippers who came to honor God found themselves haggling over prices and exchange rates before they could pray. Offerings became transactions. Reverence turned into routine. The temple's structure, though religious in appearance, had begun to erode the essence of worship.

That struck me in a personal way.

With one more family now in our circle, I found myself fixating on logistics again. Worship, once free and uncluttered, began to feel operational. I wasn't chasing money or power, but I was slipping into the same patterns, concerned with how to do things "right," when what I really needed was to return to what mattered most: the presence of God. So I began removing one thing at a time. Not out of rebellion, but out of discernment. What was helpful but not essential? What was expected but not required by Scripture? I asked myself: What is worship really made of?

The most immediate and difficult answer was money.

When I thought about church, any church, not just my own, money was always there: offerings, budgets, salaries, donations, campaigns. Even in the most sincere settings, finances shaped how things functioned. But was that the way it had to be?

So we made a decision: our small worshiping community would be free of financial transactions. No communal offering. No shared bank account. Each family would give privately, in their own way, as the Lord led them. Tithes and offerings would be collected individually and used at each family's discretion. My wife and I continued giving, supporting a struggling family during the pandemic, but we did so quietly, outside the bounds of our gathering.

Once we removed money from the equation, everything shifted. There was no more discussion about growth, expansion, or logistics. We no longer worried about building something or organizing events. Without financial ties, the temptation to measure success disappeared. We had no need for status, no urge to scale.

Jesus once said, "Destroy this temple, and in three days I will raise it up." He wasn't speaking of architecture. He was speaking of Himself. In that moment, He redefined what worship meant and where God could be found. The temple was no longer a place. It was a person. And in Him, we are being built into something new. That truth began to take root in our little gathering. We no longer saw ourselves as running a church. We were simply worshipers gathered, not organized. There was no name, no bulletin, no offering plate. But there was presence. There was peace. And most of all, there was rest.

It turns out, removing money didn't diminish our worship. It deepened it. It reminded us that ministry isn't a budget line. It's a life.

That worship doesn't need scaffolding. It needs surrender.

We still meet every week. We still open Scripture. We still pray. But now we do so with nothing to prove and nothing to maintain. We are not building something to be seen. We are becoming something unseen.

A body.
A living temple.

The church was never meant to be powered by revenue. It was meant to be sustained by love. And in this penniless community, where no one is paid and no one is owed, we have found something richer than any offering plate can hold:

A clearer glimpse of God.

Note 19
Consumption

After we removed all scheduled events and committed to just one worship service on Sundays, everything began to slow down. What had once been a packed and exhausting calendar became something simple and spacious. No matter how hectic the weekdays were, the rhythm of life grew more manageable, more human. Especially on weekends, and Sundays in particular, I found a kind of energy returning to my soul, a kind of breathing room I hadn't felt in years. I still prepared sermons and facilitated worship, but my heart was lighter, and for the first time in a long time, I experienced what felt like Sabbath rest.

And that led me to reflect more deeply: What is the Sabbath really for? What does it mean to spend the Lord's Day in a way that pleases God and restores the human soul?

Jesus' conflicts with the religious leaders often arose on the Sabbath. The Gospel of John says, "So, because Jesus was doing these things on the Sabbath, the Jewish leaders began to persecute him" (John 5:16). He healed, cast out demons, and even taught on that sacred day, acts that challenged the religious norms of His time. But Jesus made it clear: "The Sabbath was made for man, not man for the Sabbath" (Mark 2:27). He was reframing their understanding, reminding them that the Sabbath was meant to serve us, not burden us.

The roots of the Sabbath stretch back not just to the Torah, but to Genesis itself. "By the seventh day, God had finished the work he had been doing; so on the seventh day he rested from all his work"

(Genesis 2:2). Traditional interpretations view this literally, six 24-hour days of creation followed by divine rest. But that framework often collides with scientific consensus, and for many years, people have debated whether to interpret the creation story symbolically or scientifically.

In the early 2000s, I led an experimental Bible study for a group of young adults in Boston. The debate between creationism and evolution had long been a contentious issue in both church and academic circles. Rather than joining the usual back-and-forth arguments, debates that often generated more heat than light, we decided to approach the question differently. Together, we selected several books representing various perspectives: Quarks, Chaos and Christianity by John Polkinghorne, Aaron's Calf by Taek-Gyu Lim, and The Structure of Scientific Revolutions by Thomas S. Kuhn. We set a timeline, committed to reading them together, and agreed not to debate for the sake of winning a point, but to understand the foundations of each argument and examine how science and faith might speak to each other. The goal was not to declare a winner between creationism and evolution, but to wrestle with the tension honestly, and to allow each person to arrive at a reasoned, thoughtful conclusion through study, conversation, and reflection.

The outcome surprised even me.

These young adults came to an important conclusion: it was ultimately fruitless to try to force the Bible into the categories of modern science, or conversely, to stretch science until it fit neatly within the boundaries of biblical language. The two speak in fundamentally different tongues. Scripture reveals truth through story, relationship, and divine revelation. Science uncovers truth through observation, experimentation, and ever-evolving theoretical frameworks. But here's what surprised all of us: even though science and Scripture operate from different premises, the more we explored, the more we saw that science though still in progress and far from final, was not drifting away from the Bible. In fact, in many ways, it seemed to be moving toward it.

Unlike Scripture, which we believe contains a complete, inspired, and timeless truth, science is a work in progress ever learning, adjusting, and rethinking. Its discoveries are subject to revision as new tools and new perspectives emerge. And yet, as science presses deeper into the mysteries of the cosmos, it often ends up illuminating biblical truths in ways we hadn't anticipated. The young adults recognized that the more we discover about the order of the universe, the precision of its laws, the intricacy of the human body, and the structure of life itself, the more we find patterns that seem to echo the wisdom Scripture has long proclaimed.

They weren't claiming that science had suddenly proven the Bible in a definitive or mathematical way. There were still vast gaps between what science can measure and what Scripture reveals. But what they did see was a trajectory: science, rather than pulling away from faith, was inching closer. And while the distance between the two hasn't disappeared, it no longer feels like a battlefield. The gap is narrowing, and that, in itself, brought a quiet confidence. The pursuit of truth, whether in the lab or in the pages of Scripture, need not be seen as two opposing journeys, but as one converging path toward a reality larger than either discipline can fully contain.

To put it another way: science is not running away from faith, it's slowly, haltingly, running toward it.

Discoveries about the origin and fine-tuning of the universe, the symmetry and complexity of DNA, the invisible forces that govern matter and motion, all of them whisper what the Bible has declared from the beginning: "In the beginning, God created." Scholars like Francis Collins, John Polkinghorne, and others have argued that these aren't just poetic parallels, but real convergences.[16] What we observe in creation: its intentionality, order, beauty, and coherence reflects attributes we associate with God. These are not random alignments or hopeful projections. They are glimpses of the same truth through different windows. And they remind us that both science and Scripture, in their own ways, are straining to name what is ultimately beyond them: the Maker who holds it all together. So, it's not just unproductive to pit the Bible against science, it's misleading. The conflict narrative between faith and reason is based on a false dichotomy. Both are concerned with truth. Both, rightly understood, can lead us to wonder and worship.

Revisiting the Genesis creation story through this lens reveals something more profound. When we stop reading Genesis 1 as a series of literal scientific events and begin to see it as a theological and narrative expression, an ancient way of communicating the depth of God's intention in creation, we unlock a new layer of meaning. One of the most striking themes is not abrupt invention, but continuity, a flowing, ordered process. The recurring phrase, "And there was evening, and there was morning," is not merely a way to mark days; it is a poetic rhythm that reflects the harmony and sequence of divine creation. God's work is not chaotic or episodic, it unfolds with purpose and balance. And when God rests on the seventh day, it is not because He is weary, but because the creation is good, whole, and worthy of being enjoyed. This kind of rest isn't a pause, it's a celebration. And once we stop treating Genesis like a lab report and instead receive it as a sacred story rooted in divine rhythm, the idea of Sabbath as delight and fulfillment finally makes sense.

---

[16] Francis Collins, *The Language of God: A Scientist Presents Evidence for Belief* (Free Press, 2006)

That changes everything.

When we rest on the Sabbath, we are not just imitating God's inactivity, we are sharing in His joy. We are consuming the goodness He has already given. This is why Jesus healed and fed and forgave on the Sabbath, not to break the law, but to fulfill it. Every act of mercy was a continuation of God's creative and redemptive work. We were made to receive this. Our calling on the Lord's Day is not to prove ourselves through labor or service, but to receive from the One who provides.

Yet in many churches today, Sunday has become another performance. There are programs to run, events to manage, roles to fill. There is pressure to produce and perform, to keep pace, to stay relevant. We call it service, but sometimes it feels like survival. And if we step back, we realize how far this is from the Lord's original intention.

In our little community, we decided to reclaim that intention. After some reflection, we agreed on a simple principle: no events outside of worship. No extra gatherings, no planning committees, no church-wide campaigns. Just worship. Just rest. Just God. And when we made that decision, everything slowed down again.

We began to see Sunday not as a project to build, but a gift to receive. Not as a platform for our activity, but a day to consume the grace of Christ. To eat His Word. To sit in His peace. To remember that we are loved, not for what we do, but for who we are in Him. That's what the Sabbath is for. That's what the Lord's Day was always meant to be.

Not obligation, but joy. Not burden, but rest. Not performance, but presence. Not our effort, but His gift.

Note 20
Freedom in Truth

One of the most unexpected changes I experienced after stepping away from pastoral ministry and reentering the professional world was a strange but undeniable sense of peace. The corporate environment, known for its competition and relentless pace, was by no means easy, but my mind and heart felt lighter. At first, I was confused. How could I feel calmer in a world that rewards performance and punishes failure?

But in time, I realized the difference: evaluation at work, though sometimes demanding, is generally based on tangible results. There are clear expectations, and even if things don't go well, your worth as a person isn't immediately questioned. You're allowed to try, fail, learn, and try again. There is no suggestion that your character or spirituality is at fault simply because you couldn't meet a goal.

The contrast to church life was painful. The church, a place that should reflect grace, patience, and restoration, often became a setting where judgment came swiftly, and where failure, fatigue, or even healthy boundaries were interpreted as a lack of faith. The most troubling thing wasn't individual conflict, but a broader culture of scrutiny. Pastors and members alike lived under the weight of spiritualized expectations: If ministry outcomes weren't thriving, someone must be disobedient. If people weren't giving enough, praying enough, serving enough, someone's faith must be lacking.

I remember one such moment vividly. In the fall of 2019, ahead of Thanksgiving, this particular church announced a "Thanksgiving Offering Goal." For several weeks, the number was promoted, implicitly sacred, though not officially explained. After Thanksgiving Sunday, no announcement was made about whether the goal had been reached. The matter simply faded from public mention. But in the staff meeting that followed, the senior pastor publicly criticized the associate pastors calling them out by name for not giving enough. Because offerings were submitted in envelopes marked with each staff member's name, our individual contributions had been tracked. While he framed it as a concern about faith, saying our giving revealed "a lack of trust in God" and that our hearts weren't aligned with the church's mission. It was clear that the real frustration was about the shortfall. The failure to meet the offering target had become our fault. It felt less like spiritual concern and more like scapegoating.

I had given sacrificially, more than I should have, honestly. But it still wasn't enough. Not enough to satisfy someone else's standard of devotion. And that day, a question formed in my heart that I couldn't shake: Why should my faith be measured by how much I give? I realized that in this system, the metrics weren't just about money or performance, they were about proving spiritual worth. And if you didn't meet them, your devotion, even your integrity, could be quietly put on trial.

It wasn't just me. Everyone lived under pressure: volunteers, staff, and elders. There was no space for weakness. If you burned out, it was a character flaw. If your ministry didn't grow, it was faithlessness. If your offering was too small, it was disobedience. There was always something more to do, more to give, more to prove. Behind the liturgy and smiles, many of us were just anxious. Fearful. Exhausted.

That's why John 8:32 became an anchor for me: "Then you will know the truth, and the truth will set you free."

This verse lives in a chapter where Jesus confronts judgment head-on. To the woman caught in adultery, He says, "Neither do I condemn you." To the religious leaders, "You judge by human standards; I judge no one." At first glance, it seems contradictory. After all, elsewhere in Scripture Jesus is described as the one who will judge the living and the dead. So which is it?

The answer is both. Jesus does judge. But His judgment: our trial, our guilt, our sentence, has already been handed down. At the cross, the verdict was delivered. Guilty. And Jesus bore the punishment. He didn't ignore our sin; He absorbed it. He didn't cancel justice; He completed it. And because of that, we no longer live under the shadow of condemnation. The judgment has passed. We are free.

This is not abstract theology to me. It is the very truth that rescued me from shame, from fear, from the anxiety of constantly needing to justify my existence. I spent years working, serving, sacrificing, yet always wondering if it would be enough. Wondering if the church I loved would turn on me if I failed to meet expectations. Wondering if I had somehow missed God's will when results didn't come.

But now I know that Jesus does not measure my worth the way others have. He sees me as already judged, already forgiven, already loved. That truth did not just comfort me, it changed me. It released me.

And this freedom is not mine alone. It belongs to all who believe. To every pastor burdened by invisible expectations. To every layperson exhausted by guilt-based service. To every person who has sat in church and wondered, "Am I enough?"

The Church was never meant to be a factory for performance, or a theater of perfection. It was never meant to control people with shame or manipulate them with fear. It was meant to be a people of grace. A body of those who know they've been freed, and who live that freedom in love, not fear.

We are free to rest. Free to repent. Free to rise again.

When I think back on the church I served, I no longer see my departure as failure. I see it as part of a longer journey, one that is still unfolding. Like Elijah, who thought he was alone, only to learn that God had seven thousand others who had not bowed to Baal, I believe I'm not alone either. Others are walking this road. Others are waking up to the weight they've been carrying. Others are choosing truth, not pretense.

My hope is to keep walking toward the church Jesus dreamed of, a church where truth doesn't crush, but sets people free.

Author

Hank Kim

He earned his Master of Divinity from Gordon-Conwell Theological Seminary and spent over a decade serving in church leadership and pastoral ministry in both Boston and New York City. He now leads a small worshiping community rooted in simplicity and sincerity. His professional journey began at Samsung Electronics in 1995, launching a career in marketing that later expanded into consulting across sectors such as education, wellness, and healthcare. Today, he continues his work as a consultant and writer at GW Creative.

Bibliography

TEXT

1. Collins, Francis, The Language of God: A Scientist Presents Evidence for Belief (Free Press, 2006).
2. Duffy, Eamon, The voices of Morebath: Reformation and rebellion in an English village (Yale University Press, 1997).
3. Grenz, Stanley & Olson, Roger 20th century theology: God and the world in a transitional age (InterVarsity Press, 1992, Downers Grove, IL).
4. Hamilton, Victor P., The book of Genesis: Chapters 1-17, Vol. 1 (Wm. B. Eerdmans Publishing., 1990).
5. Jensen, Richard A., The Widow's Offering: A Theology of Giving (Wm. B. Eerdmans Publishing Co., 1996).
6. Kinnaman, David & Lyon, Gabe, You Lost Me: Why Young Christians Are Leaving Church . . . and Rethinking Faith (Bakers Book, 2016).
7. Kroeger, Catherine, The Woman at the Well: A Different Look (Augsburg Fortress. 1992).
8. Lewis, Jacqueline, "Empathy and Zacchaeus: A Lesson from Jesus" Journal of Religious Thought (72(1), 2016).
9. Meeks Wayne A., The Economic World of Early Christianity (Yale University Press, 1989).
10. Raymond, William D., The Basilica and the Cathedral in the Early Christian West (Ashgate Publishing Company, 2003).

INTERNET

11. Boffey, Matthew "5 Insights for Interpreting the Deaths of Ananias and Sapphira" Logos (May 2021, https://www.logos.com/grow/5-insights-for-interpreting-the-deaths-of-ananias-and-sapphira/).
12. Bush, Luis, "A Brief Historical Overview of the AD2000 & Beyond Movement and Joshua Project 2000"Luisbush Papers (May 1996, https://luisbushpapers.com/joshua-project/1995/11/01/a-brief-historical-overview-of-the-ad2000-movement-and-joshua-project-2000/).
13. Gabbatt, Adam, "Losing their religion: why US churches are on the decline"The Guardian (January 2023, https://www.theguardian.com/us-news/2023/jan/22/us-churches-closing-religion-covid-christianity).
14. Pack, David C., "The True Meaning of Lent,"The Restored Church of God (https://rcg.org/articles/ttmol.html).
15. Wang, Wendy, "Here's Who Stopped Going to Church During the Pandemic" Christianity Today (January 2022, https://www.christianitytoday.com/ct/2022/january-web-only/attendance-decline-covid-pandemic-church.html).

GWCreative
Good-Will makes a difference

www.ingramcontent.com/pod-product-compliance
Lightning Source LLC
Chambersburg PA
CBHW060336050426
42449CB00011B/2774